I0261176

Praise for *Diary of Small Discontents*

Across the amazing & ever-changing arc of John Yau's poetry the range of possibility, steeped in sound, image, story's insistent edges, every formal variation available, and something like total word love, is vast and exact. Sonnets may be Broken, Egyptian or O Pin Yin, adjacent to A Painter's Thoughts and Morning Thoughts, overlapping with Russian Letters, the tales of Ghengis Chan, Adventures in Monochrome, and Black Threads from Meng Chiao, these serial studies of character and mind. In John Yau's poems the sense—my sense—of presence is always multiple, amused amidst difficult questions, and unremitting. Consciousness comes forward to recede and reform again, changed by experience and attraction. Emotive tones may be inseparable from personae: voices in their various costumes listened to in chaotic order to try on, channeled from an endless stream of vessels, i.e. the mournful necessities of respect and need, rich with humor so as to continue. *Diary of Small Discontents*, a half century-long picture-wild adventure, is a major gift to anyone capable of loving poetry. —ANSELM BERRIGAN

Acclaimed poet, artist and art critic John Yau dazzles us with his *Diary of Small Discontents: New and Selected Poems 1977–2024*. Whether it's the early poem with a child playing on the stoop in "After Moving," or the late pantoum/elegy "For Brice Marden (1938–2023) via Han Shan," Yau's range of expressive moods and moves is extraordinary. The humor, Basho or Baboo inflected, parodic, hews to the music. Feel the tension reading the steamy, dreamy 16th century Christopher Marlowe appropriation, "Come live with me," in Yau's "Ill-Advised Love Poem" or the poignant urgency in "Black Threads from Meng Chaio 2"—"Spring left when / I was not looking." Or in "Borrowed Love Poems," "what can I do, now that I've sent you / a necklace of dead bees," from Mandelshtam's "necklace fashioned of dead bees." Prismatic observation of paintings, as in "Written in the Shadows Cast by *The Burning of the Houses of Lords and Commons* (1835) by J. M. W. Turner" colors sublime poems. Conversations with painters themselves give rise to the balanced beauty of "Ventriloquist for Jasper Johns" or the finely wrought series, "A Painter's Thoughts." Yau's acute, incisive wit is unflinching. Behind the wit is a gravity, a kind of radiant compassion with a flinty blade, as in "On Being Told That I Don't Look and Act Chinese." The wry, contradictory mix of issues like race, class, "the headman . . . the deadman," is compelling. John Yau's speculative koans operate to puzzle conceptual thought. His irresistible *Diary of Small Discontents* is the enduring conversation that we seek. —NORMA COLE

Taking seriously the concept that "content is merely the extension of form," John Yau is a supreme formalist. He creates an integrity of structure that allows him to go anywhere in his poetry and he does in the most surprising and original ways. The work never ceases to surprise. His poetry is at once buoyant and piercing, funny and dark. Very dark. Very funny. John Yau is also an important and extraordinary precursor to contemporary Asian American poetry. His long-standing career and voluminous adventurous writing attests to his masterful achievement. *Diary of Small Discontents: New and Selected Poems 1974–2024* is essential reading for essential poets. —PETER GIZZI

Also by John Yau

POETRY

Sometimes (1979)
Broken Off by the Music (1981)
Corpse and Mirror (1983)
Radiant Silhouette: New & Selected Work 1974–1988 (1989)
Big City Primer (1991), with photographs by Bill Barrette
Edificio Sayonara (1992)
Berlin Diptychon (1995), with photographs by Bill Barrette
Forbidden Entries (1996)
Borrowed Love Poems (2002)
Ing Grish (2005), with Thomas Nozkowski
Paradiso Diaspora (2006)
Further Adventures in Monochrome (2012)
Bijoux in the Dark (2018)
Genghis Chan on Drums (2021)
Tell It Slant (2023)

FICTION

The Sleepless Night of Eugene Delacroix (1980)
Hawaiian Cowboys (1995)
My Symptoms (1996)
My Heart Is That Eternal Rose Tattoo (2001)

CRITICISM

The Passionate Spectator: Essays on Art and Poetry (2006)
The Wild Children of William Blake (2017)
Foreign Sounds or Sounds Foreign (2020)
Please Wait by the Coat Room: Reconsidering Race and Identity in American Art (2023)

COLLABORATIONS

100 More Jokes from the Book of the Dead (2001), with Archie Rand

MONOGRAPHS

In the Realm of Appearances: The Art of Andy Warhol (1993)
A. R. Penck (1993)
Ed Moses: A Retrospective of Paintings and Drawings, 1951–1996 (1996)
The United States of Jasper Johns (1996)
Pat Steir: Dazzling Water, Dazzling Light (2001)
Joan Mitchell: Works on Paper 1956–1992 (2007)
A Thing Among Things: The Art of Jasper Johns (2008)
William Tillyer: Watercolours (2010)
Jay DeFeo: Chiaroscuro (2013)
Richard Artschwager: Into the Desert (2015)
Catherine Murphy (2016)
Thomas Nozkowski (2017)
California Landscapes: Richard Diebenkorn / Wayne Thiebaud (2018)
Philip Taaffe (2018)
William Tillyer: A Retrospective (2021)
Liu Xiaodong (2021)
Joe Brainard: The Art of the Personal (2022)

EDITOR

The Collected Poems of Fairfield Porter (1985), with David Kermani
Fetish (1998)

JOHN YAU

DIARY OF SMALL DISCONTENTS

New & Selected Poems 1974–2024

OMNIDAWN PUBLISHING
OAKLAND, CALIFORNIA
2025

Cover art by Judy Linn, "fish, East Broadway" (1995), photograph in gelatin silver print, 16" x 20". By permission of the artist.
Cover and interior design by Shanna Compton

Cover typeface: Museo Sans
Interior typefaces: Adobe Garamond Pro and Museo Sans

Library of Congress Cataloging-in-Publication Data

Names: Yau, John, 1950- author
Title: Diary of small discontents : new & selected poems 1974-2024 / John Yau.
Other titles: Diary of small discontents (Compilation)
Description: Oakland, California : Omnidawn Publishing, 2025. | Summary: "This collection brings together work from half a century of writing by John Yau. Preoccupied with forms and musical structures, Yau's work includes sestinas, sonnets, pantoums, and lists, as well as invented forms. Employing both strict and open-ended frameworks, Yau creates multi-faceted poems that can shift abruptly from humor to outrage and consider topics including Chinese American identity, school shootings, invented countries, and haunted memories. Some poems are grounded in an autobiographical voice, while others take on the voices of other characters, including contemporary artists and a fictional Chinese private eye. Spanning the vast diversity of Yau's forms and subjects, the poems in Diary of Small Discontents add up to an unapologetically original collection"-- Provided by publisher.
Identifiers: LCCN 2025017469 (print) | LCCN 2025017470 (ebook) | ISBN 9781632431752 trade paperback | ISBN 9781632431981 ebook
Subjects: LCGFT: Poetry
Classification: LCC PS3575.A9 D53 2025 (print) | LCC PS3575.A9 (ebook) | DDC 811/.54--dc23/eng/20250527
LC record available at https://lccn.loc.gov/2025017469
LC ebook record available at https://lccn.loc.gov/2025017470

Published by Omnidawn Publishing, Oakland, California
www.omnidawn.com
10 9 8 7 6 5 4 3 2 1
ISBN: 978-1-63243-175-2

for Joe Donahue

In my heart I am Chinese, and I am going home.

—Franz Kafka

Contents

Section 5 (2013–2020)

Section 6 (2021–2023)

Section 1
(1974–1988)

After Moving

Even as the street becomes familiar to you;
        almost incidental
the way details in novels can add
        immovable color
to the overall scheme; and the faces pass
        from strangers to companions
without the intervention of touch; and the traffic
        no longer sounds harsh,
but instead grows muted as the gray afternoons
        that occasionally fill
the sky with a festering sun behind clouds
        rubbed smooth;
you feel removed from the surrounding scenery,
        though if you were asked,
you would not deny you have a place in this
        circumstance, and partake of
events; though they rarely, if ever,
        seem as connected as the streets do;
angles of one block joined to another,
        the buildings jammed
together, with a child playing on the stoop;
        or covering her eyes
while her friends run into the darkness
        the game takes into account

The Reading of an Ever-Changing Tale

Certain colors got lodged under
our fingernails before their names
came to grace our speech. But
what of the phenomena whose
colors can only be imagined?
What did you do with the pills?
And why were you without any gasoline?
Today, these questions are a restraint
on your memory as the color
"blue" is a box opened up
like a sky under which
no grass grows. But traces remain.
The war you only just heard about
inextricably mixed with a face
you will probably never see again.

Ten Songs

Trying to find a way to say something that would make it make its sense
Trying to find a way to weigh something that would make its own lens
Finding a way to say something they would make a lens of
Finding the saying of something, weighing the sense of it trying
Making the trying something that would find its sense
Sensing the making trying to find something it says
Saying the finding is there to find is making it make sense
Making it make sense is finding something to say
Something to say is finding a lens to sense the making
Something making the making something something else

Cameo of a Chinese Woman on Mulberry Street

Her face this moon a house
Always nearing the end of its road

From within each room
Rising rising

Slowly up through their sleep
For a breath

The pale fur and dark wings
The silver beak and silver talons

Robert Herrick

I like wallpaper that makes sense.

I own and operate a gas station
that stands neatly clustered on a wedge
formed by a fork in the road.
The dust is a hindrance, but not a veil.

Even on overcast days I can see my face
like the shell of a scooped-out cantaloupe
rising in the windshields.
And sometimes at night, I can see its ellipse
floating toward me, as if
what it was going to say this time
would make today a departure
from all the rest.

In the afternoon the lake is as smooth
as the polished black hood
of Mr. Meriwether's vintage '38 Cadillac.
It has that bottomless dark feeling about it
that only cars and lakes and you can have.

Chinese Villanelle

I have been with you, and I have thought of you
Once the air was dry and drenched with light
I was like a lute filling the room with description

We watched glum clouds reject their shape
We dawdled near a fountain and listened
I have been with you, and I have thought of you

Like a river worthy of its gown
And like a mountain worthy of its insolence
Why am I like a lute, left with only description

How does one cut an axe handle with an axe
What shall I do to tell you all my thoughts
When I have been with you and dreamt of you

A pelican sits on a dam, while a duck
Folds its wings again; the song does not melt
I remember you looking at me without description

Perhaps an emperor's business is never finished
Though "perhaps" implies a different beginning.
I have been with you and I have schemed with you
Now I am a lute filled with this wandering description

From Scenes from the Life of Boullée

1.

Roof shaped like a strawberry. Hurriedly torn
paper towel. The queen's staircase does not
lead to the king's chambers. The traditional
requirements of comfort and convenience.
A kind of sleepwalking echoed by a line
in history. Stands on a lovesick giant
and calls himself a hero. Sound of annoyance
at an unforeseen circumstance becoming an
inevitable consequence. Wine dripping off
the Formica table onto the shag rug after
hitting the unused wooden chair covered
with cigarette burns. A dream heard
second hand. An extra coat hanger.
Only half the story is true. The rest
is necessary, like clouds on a cloudy day.

2.

Pieces of a piece. The face in the window larger
than the window facing in. A mermaid selling
cheese in a laundromat in Ottawa. A cop who looks
as if he has to go to the bathroom. A bony hand
dangling from a red station wagon. Riding in a cab
with a junkie who wants an alarm clock. Breaking
a promise and counting the pieces. Her harsh

lipstick crumbling over her harsher smile.
Remnants of a collision in a galaxy whose
name is a number. Eeriness of a city with
only one streetlight. The kinds of certainty
available in a drugstore. Jumbo food.
with only one light on. A junkie dangling
from an alarm clock. Using the laundromat
because there were no bathrooms around.
Stealing the mermaid's cheese. Breaking
into her smile. The kinds of certainty
available in a supermarket, a newspaper,
a lover. A young cop who looks as if he
has gone. The square face in the round
window. Pieces of a blue piece.

3.

Without noticing the fire descending into the
subway station. Descending into the copper
sunlight. Going back again and again.
Their voices. One dripping. The other dribbling
to a stop. Lengthening each of the sounds into
a staircase. I think there's three volumes.
A salmon. A sale's on. Ceylon. Existence
being the only record of their names.
Shoes seen by the side of the highway
leading to Las Vegas. Faces remembered
from last Thursday. Talking to an imaginary
friend in your sleep. Waking up and feeling
the sweat. The sweet surrounding your skin.
Adding to the pile. The only thing invisible

for miles. In every kind of light. The light
of topless dancing. Only half of you is there.
No music sparring with traffic. Enters
in a suit the color of coffee, face the color
of masking tape. Everyone looks like you, today.
Even people I don't like.

Late Night Movies I

In a small underground laboratory the brain of a
movie actor is replaced by semiprecious stones,
each one thought to have once resided in heaven.

An archaeologist realized the inside of an ancient
mask carried a picture of satin meant only for its
dead inhabitant. A nurse walks into a hospital
and knew something was missing.

In the afternoon, rain washed away all traces
of the railroad station. A crow hid its head
under its wing. A tourist sneezed twice and
wondered if there was any truth to the legend
inscribed over the doorway of the pharmacy

Beware the opinions of a dead movie,
an empty hospital and a wounded crow
        on a rainy afternoon,
a missing brain and a train station built beside a river,
a nurse carrying a photograph of heaven.

In a small laboratory in heaven the semiprecious thoughts
of a movie star are replaced by a brain.
The ancient mask realized the insides of the
archaeologist exuded a tincture of *Pisa*
meant only for its dead inhabitant

Outside the train station the nurse wondered if
there was any truth to the legend inscribed
around the rims of her new tires. The brain
of the movie actor is carried by a tourist.

In a small underground temple, the wing of a crow
is replaced by semiprecious stones, each one
thought to have been a sneeze from heaven.

The nurse hid the hands of Orpheus under a painting
of a train station, whose shadow reached the river
where all legends began. A doctor realized the
doorway of the pharmacy was missing. A woman
wondered why a picture of heaven had replaced her tires.
The movie actor's only desire was to be seen
by the dead, to be fixed in the lining
of the clouds gathered over their grave

The archaeologist slept in a hospital with
as many windows as days in the year and wondered
if there was any truth to the legend inscribed
on the semiprecious stones the tourist carried
across the plaza in the afternoon rain

At times, the nurse thought the only desires
Were the ones without names

The head of Orpheus floated down the river, leaving
behind the hospital, were, as one version
of the legend claimed, the song would continue
forever in the hallways leading to the sea.

Late Night Movies II

Gone with the wind. What remains of the charred
toolbox is something the detective cannot get
off his mind.

Through the dirty window, down an alley strewn with
identifiable pieces of garbage, toward the doorway
of a rundown hotel. Bits fly back.

Snores rise through the rafters of the sagging barn.
The creature crawls out of the swamp, and begins
walking around the campfire. Introduces a blonde,
a smile, and a promise.

Done with the wing. He cannot scrape the detective's
charred remains off the tool box. The blonde smiles,
combs her hairs, and then lights a cigarette in the
deserted bus station. Identifiable pieces
of the creature fly back through the dirty window.

An itch in time staves nine. The blonde smiles,
combs her cigarette, and then lights
his sagging swamp on fire. What remains of the
detective crawls past the dirty window.

Stalk walls and carry a big tick. Perhaps
the creature will turn in time to keep his
throat intact, his snores identifiable.

The bomb continues its countdown in an aisle.
A child opens his hand over and over. What
remains of the tool box rises through
the rafters of a sagging hotel.
Introduces a snore, crawls out of a smile,
scrapes an itch, combs the throat.

Don't wire until you see the fights of their eyes.
Introduced in the doorway of a hotel. Pine tree
moonlight. Tonight, a bird in the band is worth
two in the hush; the hush surrounding
a lifetime of guarantees.

Late Night Movies III

1.

The headman did the right thing. He displayed
his wit, as they watched the snow from a bench
in the park. However, when the weather cleared,
Rimbaud knew his boss would order the dogs to
continue hauling the men to paradise.

The dead man hid the right thing. He displayed
his bit, as they snatched the woe from a wench
in the park. However, when the weather cleared,
Baudelaire knew his boss would order the dogs to
continue mauling the hen to paradise.

2.

Rimbaud was alone when he picked up the tongs
and stood by the side of the river. A bad planner,
he carried his first marriage into the mountains,
where she would burn his toast to ashes every
morning. But tonight, during the late night movies,
he listened for the hush coming from the gate.

Baudelaire was alone when he picked up the songs
and stood by the tide of the river. A plaid banner.
He married his first carriage into the mountains,
where she would turn his boast to ashes every
morning. And tonight, during the mate night lovies,
he heard the gush coming from the hate.

3.

In the market place Rimbaud watched and followed
them. An old man and his wife wanted their son
to trade for gold. All the wheat they harvested
for a tiny bag of radiant specks. By the end of
the afternoon both of them were hurrying in front of
the waiting salesman.

In the market place, Baudelaire watched and followed
them. An old man and his young wife wanted to trade their son
for gold. All the heat they had saved had harvested
this tiny radiant speck. By the end of the afternoon
however, both of them were worrying in front
of the hating salesman.

4.

After he fled the mountain fired with autumn,
Rimbaud preferred sleeping in the corner of the
library, and, later, washing his hands in the
park. He was tired of unloading baskets of
canned meat for the butchers of Toledo.
When it rains, it pours, he thought. And
He wanted to move up from sardines and crumbs.

After he left the fountain mired with autumn,
Baudelaire preferred weeping in a corner of the
library and, later, slashing his hands in the
park. He was tired of unloading caskets of
banned meat for the butchers of Toledo.
When it pains, it roars, he thought. And
he wanted to arrive with carbines and drums.

5.

The rain began pushing him back into the hospital.
After months of washing their dirty dishes, Rimbaud
knew he had to leave this infernal house of death
or perish. The skies would clear, but there was
still a sense of doom in the air, as he glanced
out the open window, hoping the next time he would leave forever.
The pain began rushing him back into the hospital.
After months of dashing their dirty wishes, Baudelaire
knew he had to leave this infernal louse of death
or perish. The skies had cleared, but there was
still a sense of gloom in the air, as he danced
out the open window, hoping the next time he would cleave forever.

Shanghai Shenanigans

The moon empties its cigarette over a row of clouds
whose window sills tremble in the breeze

The breeze pushed my boat through a series
of telephone conversations started by perfume

Perfume splashed over the words of a nomad
who believed it was better to starve than laugh

To laugh over the administration's most recent gaffe
will make the guests stay until the party

Until the party is bundled in chatter
I will count the pearls lingering around your neck

The Dream Life of a Coffin Factory in Lynn, Massachusetts

Earlier in the century it was not unusual to spend an evening on the verandah.
It was a time when movie theaters sprawled around
newly constructed lagoons, their blue concrete walls
rising out of Wisconsin snow drifts, their tile roofs
fiercely gathering Delaware's windswept soot in March.

Every street personalized its drugstores with mahogany stools
on which one could perch, and wait for evening to unfold its
        newspaper, shake out its umbrella.
And at night, long after everyone was asleep,
the rows of chrome spigots still gleamed with pride.

Now it was dusk; and floating above these warm suburbs
was a tremendous dome, whose perimeter was molded
with high relief figures of motorcycles and pouting dancers,
wagon wheels and other things classical.

In Wisconsin's lagoons it was still considered graceful
for a man to sit in a drugstore and wait for a hand to squeeze an orange pill.

In Delaware's soot a woman could sit on a wall
and lose hours counting clouds unfolding in the darkness.

It was, if anything, a newly constructed century—
a time when only motorcycles sprawled fiercely in the rain.

Behind the movie theater a warm glow spread out
from the window of the hacienda, bravely gathering
the remnants of evening to its yellow handkerchief.

Even the narrower streets had their own lagoons,
each one lined with stucco clouds on which one could sleep,
waiting for evening to deliver its pastel uniforms.
It would remain an evening of waiting,
for men and omen floated above the suburbs,
pouting fiercely in the last stages of a withered century.

In March, in Wisconsin, young men shed their moustaches.
        After carefully weighing them,
they were placed in linen handkerchiefs ad buried in the snow.
In the evening they ran back to the classical suburbs,
where rows of young women leaned in glistening drugstores,
waiting for the clouds to get older.

The perimeter of these suburbs was carefully outlined by chrome spigots.
Lawns rose fiercely out of the snow, while paper bags seldom crossed the avenue.
If a newspaper floated past the window, a pale hand clutched a withered foot.
It was a time when the century had gone to sleep,
and everyone glistened with pride.

Broken Off by the Music

With the first gray light of dawn the remnants
of gas stations and supermarkets assume their
former shapes. A freckled, redheaded boy
stares into the refrigerator, its chrome shelves
lined with jars, cans, and bottles—each
appropriately labeled with a word and a picture.
For some of the other inhabitants of the yellow
apartment house, the vapor of food in the morning
is sufficient nourishment.

Along the highway dozens of motorists have pulled
onto the shoulder of the road, no longer guided
by the flicker of countless stars dancing over
the surface of the asphalt. Three radios
disagree over what lies ahead. It is morning,
and sand no longer trickles onto the austere
boulevards of the capital.

Outside, on the sidewalk, two girls kneel down
and pray in front of a restaurant closed for
vacation. A breeze reminds everyone that ice
is another jewel—the result of snow gleaming
at night. "I used to play on this street,
but now it is different," says the older girl.
The younger one, who might be her sister, nods
solemnly. Across the street is a store
no one will enter.

Distance can hardly lend enchantment to the remnants
of a supermarket where faces are torn, as always,
between necessity and desire. With the first gray
light of evening a freckled girl assumes her former
shape—each limb appropriately labeled with words
of instruction. The younger boy skips away from
the others, while singing a song full of words
he stumbles over.

Outside the capital, two motorists disagree over
the remnants of a refrigerator. Three boys stare
at what lies behind the stars. A breeze reminds
everyone of their former shapes, while evening
lends an austere enchantment to the yellow window of a gas station.
Snow can hardly provide enchantment to a sidewalk
where two girls shiver uncontrollably,
while looking for the doorway of a store
that is closed. Nearby, a woman labels
gray shapes with songs of disagreement.

Three supermarkets disagree over the food vapors
in a refrigerator. Along the highway the sand
becomes a song of chrome enchantment. A young boy
kicks the remnants of his brother's radio.

"I used to pray on this street, but now it is
sufficient to return each afternoon," he whispers,
as if someone were listening.

A woman stops in front of a gas station and stares
at the surface of the stars drifting though the
clouds. The breeze reminds the motorist that

the first light of dawn is the remnant of a jewel.

Thousands of radios begin flickering throughout
the apartment complex.

The shoulders of the younger sister are covered
with snow. The sidewalk in front of the restaurant
is littered with sleeping motorists, each of them
fixated on the breeze trickling through the clouds.
But at night, the sky is a window full of earrings,
each lost in its blue velvet box.

Two boys nod solemnly in front of their former shapes.
Someone has embroidered the remnants of enchantment.

Corpse and Mirror (I)

1.

When one of our citizens dies, his corpse is placed in his chariot. To help him reach his destination, his favorite horses are buried with him.

By the time dawn breaks out of its cage in the mountains, the gravediggers have gently lowered the chariot and its contents into the pit. Now, the horses must be rounded up and measured with the precision of a tailor. For each of these nervous engines must fit smoothly into its own grave, so only the head with its fearful yet fiery eyes emerge above the ground, like a hand rising from the sea.

Once the gravediggers have accomplished this task, they return immediately to the city. Their pace is quickened by the knowledge that inside their kitchens steam has started rising from the glistening slabs of meat, tureens of brightly colored vegetables, and baskets of earth-colored breads.

All afternoon they have dreamed of entering a room like this, full of solace and celebration. And yet, when each of them reaches the door, they hesitate; almost as if they wished they could join the procession of heads towing an invisible cargo toward the setting sun, the next city that must be reached before dawn escapes once more.

If a man's sins outweigh his acts of kindness, the horses will eventually collapse and blood will stream from their nostrils. Beneath the moon the man will revive, but he will have become so hideously ugly since his last breath left him that no one—not even the most generous of Samaritans—will be able to offer him food and shelter. He will remain in this condition, doomed to wander in the desert like a vulture without wings.

The only way he will be given another chance is if one of his neighbors dreams about him in the week following his death. In the dream, the dead man must give his exact location beneath the stars. At dawn, the neighbor must ride out to the spot and see if he is there. If he isn't, the kindhearted neighbor must dismount at once and begin praying, for he has been deceived once again. Death has not stopped the deceased from continuing along the path he chose in life. If the neighbor does not pray at once, he must surrender all hope of ever finding his way back to the city. The dead man has chosen him for a companion, and he has been foolish enough to accept.

2.

When one of our citizens dies, his head is cut off and placed inside a mirror-lined box. The box is tightly sealed, allowing no light to enter its interior, and placed in the least used room in the house. Each night someone must sleep beside the varnished cube in which the head resides. After two weeks have elapsed, the box can be interred beside the rest of the corpse.

However, if everyone in the family bears a grudge against the deceased, an anger so deep that death has not removed its poison, they may burn the box and joyfully kick the ashes and bone fragments into the river. The decision must be reached without ever being mentioned. Finally, once the ashes begin floating downstream, the deceased's name can never be brought up in conversation again.

Once the head is inside the box, the eyelids will push against the weight of dreams and sleep until they open. It will never occur to him that his head has been severed from his body. Instead, he will believe he has been kidnapped and buried in the sand. Before him is a road stretching to the horizon. Above him the moon patrols the walls of its vast domain. Escape is impossible. By morning the vultures will begin circling patiently.

Soon he begins rambling, imagining his mouth is parched and full of sand. This is a signal. Whoever is sleeping in the room must awaken immediately and begin listening to the voice echoing inside the box. What happens next depends on who has died. If instructions are uttered, they must be followed faithfully. If a confession is made, it must be heard without judgment. Whatever is said must be kept a secret.

If you are sent to another city, you must saddle your horse at dawn and leave without speaking to anyone. Once you are there, you must find the house the voice described. A house similar to all the houses on all the winding streets in this haphazardly designed city, and yet different in one essential way. When the door opens you will know why. However, if the person who answers the door is puzzled by your request, then you have failed to listen to the instructions carefully enough. In this case, you must return to your house without speaking to anyone along the way. No one in your family will greet you. You cannot sleep beside the box again, but must remain inside your room until the two weeks is over.

One night, after the box has been buried or burned, you will hear something outside your window, inside your dream. The words may not be words at all, but the fluttering of a bird caught in a snare. A broken pot. A bucket falling into a well. Listen carefully. He may need to speak to you once again.

No One Ever Tried to Kiss Anna May Wong

She's trying to find a way to turn her cup
upside down, while sequestered on a train
from Dublin to Vienna. Every angle
glistens from behind a celluloid scrim.
She's wearing a crescent scarf
and chilly snake high smile:
others claim she's all skin and eyes.
No longer lashed to this oily chatter
I enter her compartment.

She's languishing
on a ledge, annoyed at all the times
she's been told to be scratched, kicked,
slapped, bitten, stabbed, poisoned, and shot.
Lightning flickers between the frames.
On the seat beside me I find a circle
smaller than one left by a wet apple.

Genghis Chan: Private Eye I

I was floating through a cross section
with my dusty wine glass, when she entered,
a shivering bundle of shredded starlight.
You don't need words to tell a story,
a gesture will do. These days,
we're all parasites looking for a body
to cling to. I'm nothing more
than riffraff splendor drifting past the runway.
I always keep a supply of lamprey lipstick around,
just in case.
                    She laughed,
A slashed melody of small shrugs.
It had been raining in her left eye.
She began: a cloud or story
broken in two maybe four places,
wooden eyelids, and a scarf of human hair.
She paused: I offer you dervish bleakness
and glistening sediment.
                                        It was late
and we were getting jammed in deep.
I was on the other side, staring at
the snow-covered moon pasted above the park.
A foul lump started making promises in my voice.

Genghis Chan: Private Eye III

We surfed out of the alley,
the stories our parents told us
trailing behind, like angry yellow toads

You spoke first:
One of my ancestral coupons
composed the bulldozer anthem
Perhaps she too was waiting
for the bumper crop showers
to subside, another dust mote picker
in a long line of lovelorn imports
Yes, I too was stymied by the animal of music
and the shadow its breath sent through history

I wanted to tell you
about the bank teller and the giant,
the red moths hovering above their heads

I wanted to tell you
About the gizmo pit and kinds of sludge
I have cataloged during my investigation

I wanted to tell you
about how the sun
dissolved all of this long ago

leaving us in different rooms

registered under different names

Genghis Chan: Private Eye VI

I am just another particle cloud gliding across the screen

A swamp chanter doodling on the margins of the abyss

I prefer rat backs to diplomatic curls

I am the owner of one pockmarked tongue

I park it on the hedge between sure bets and bad business

Genghis Chan: Private Eye XIX

My stamped mother
used to fling to me

All Stones lead to the home
Go easy on the turtle pie

gored down
at doom temperature

Cast a cold
and dirty style

on every yellow
leaf of lassitude

glistening beneath
the grappled fly

My stamped mother
used to fling to me

and I
her lump of muck

would fling back
all the riveted bones

I could dandle
on my wasted plea

the chink of meat
we knew that linked us

to the junk
going by

Genghis Chan: Private Eye XXXIX

(Seventh Ideogram)

DISGUISE

———

THE LIMIT

Inuit Villanelle

For John Lees

If this is the word, how did you know it?
Whale is good, but caribou is better.
Did you change your mind? Or did you lose it?

Can you chop ice? Have you sharpened it?
I stare at the rotting stump until supper.
If this is the place, how will I show it?

Will you mash the berries? Would you like to sit?
I never went fishing with him or his brother.
Did I change my mind? Or did I lose it?

I washed my parka and sewed the mitt.
I cannot make it go any faster.
If this is the way, I will learn to use it.

I have drawn the stump. Would you like to see it?
You must tell me the original name of the river.
If this is the word, how will I know it?
Did you change your mind? Or did I lose it?

Modern Love

The clouds continued swelling like poisoned fish
While the boy listened carefully to the story
That was being invented by the girl
Who, like him, had been abandoned in the city.
They were, she whispered, itchy to avoid the forest
And reach the little red motel by the stream.

However, when she came to the edge of the stream,
She began trembling like a fish.
She was going to have to leave the forest,
After all, and hear the birds cackling at the recital of her story.
"I've become as soft and defenseless as a drug-infested city.
I might as well eat rags and dust," muttered the girl.

Suddenly, the boy was scared of the girl
And wondered how to cover the stream
Of invectives she was leaving all over their city
Owned apartment: perhaps if I steal a fish
Pick some flowers, and beg you to finish the story,
You will remember how to lead us past the forest.

Remembering that no one had ever circumnavigated the forest
Before, she tried to pretend she was just another pretty but deranged girl.
"Don't be afraid: If you happen to fall off the edge of my story,
Remember that paper is made from trees that have crashed into a stream
It is only frightening if you are a fish."
She put on her best stupid smile and looked out at the city

Which had spread further than any other city.
Still, no one had been able to map the forest.
"Before you go out and catch a fish,
I should teach you how to swim," said the girl.
"There is something lurking at the bottom of the stream
And it may attempt to break into my story."

This happens every time she tells a story,
He thought, as evening's shadows absorbed the city.
I can no longer be sure of the meaning of "stream."
Or what is immeasurable about the forest.
If I am lucky, I will be able to convince next girl
That life's pleasures consist of warm rows of oily fish.

"Actually, the story is about two fish
Who leave their stream to live in the forest
It is a parable about our life in the city," began the girl.

Section 2
(1989–1995)

First and Last Views (I)

It is the icing on the cake, the nation's thyroid
gland, a beautiful catastrophe. There are roughly
three New Yorks. Hatted, feathered, and flounced.
You have to be on a bridge to enjoy it.
Pyramid on pyramid like a white cloud-head
above a thunderstorm. It rises like Venice.
A giant asparagus bed of alabaster and rose
green skyscrapers. City of prose, fantasy, and
automatic fire. A pincushion in profile.
An enormous system of shuttles and bobbins.
Token of cluster. Last word until another word
is written, vocabulary of thrift. Mad dance of
inanimate matter, twentieth century's Rosetta Stone.
Covered with yellow foam and seamed with
wrinkles. Littered with chips, shavings, straw,
remains of food. A stomach that has swallowed
several million people, busily grinding and digesting
enormous worms wriggle along, dragging
cars behind them. Three thousand swords
shine through the soft swan of mist.
A huge rich raisin as opposed to a flat wide pie.
South and north of the sunset pit.

New York Map Company (1)

Acton Town Manufacturing
Beyond the Bosphorus
Cyprus Minerals
Denver Fire Clay
Eldorado Cleaner
Fresno Touch
Glasgow Botanica
Hanover Head
Illinois Bronze Powder and Paint
Jerusalem Cooling
Kitty Hawk Industries
London Towne House
Malts Drydocks
Nottingham Shoes
Osaka Shiatsu Spa
Pompei Construction
Quincy Compressor
Rio Grande Exchange
Seoul Shoe Repair and Dry Cleaning
Timbuctoo Timbers
Uranus Sunshine
Venezuela Auto Repair
Warsaw Electric
Xanadu Labs
Yukon Trails Division
Zanzibar Courier Service

New York Map Company (2)

Amsterdam Air Cooling
Brasil Contempo
Center City Planning
Dullsville Incorporated
Edo Antiques
Fur Town Cleaners
Globe Master Locksmith
Hellenic Wiring
Igloo Social Club
Jupiter Legal Video Communications
Kansas Advertising Limited
Lourdes Pharmacy
Malibu Pet Hotel
Ninth Circle Psychotherapy Referral
Oasis Capital
Pyrenees Mountain Clock
Queensland Quick Step Supply
Ruhr of Brooklyn
Sphinx Transportation
Trafalgar Business Systems
Universe Grocery Store
Valley Forge Snowmobile Repair
Walla Walla Concepts
Xingcheng Trading Company
Yap Island Shirts
Zacatecas Refining

A Is for Automobile

Cimarron is a luxury specialty, in the same class as
Toronado, Seville, and Eldorado. In the New World,
cimarron was first used to designate runaway cattle.
Later, it meant "escaped slaves."

In Spanish, Nova is "No va" and means, "It doesn't go."

El Dorado was a legendary city of gold purported by
various indigenous people to be somewhere in
South America. In Spanish, the name means
"the gilded one."

Birds, Stones, Planets, Cities, and streets

Birthplace of Napoleon.

A kind of handgun.

A French each and a French general.

A sea bird.

A chief of the Ottawa; a city in Michigan.
Between 1600 and 1663, the fur trade
moved up the St. Lawrence and Ottawa Rivers.

The Greek god of commerce, travel, and thievery,
who serves as messenger of the gods; the smallest planet

Of those near the sun; a silvery-white poisonous metallic
element that is liquid at room temperature and is used
in thermometers and chemical pesticides.

A man chosen to represent his country.

It is derived from the Old English word for "camel."

Any number of devices that use radiating properties
of systems or molecules to generate light; the amplification
of light in which all waves are polarized and exactly aligned.

From the Tupi word meaning "to run like a deer."
Destructive natural force.

Positions and descriptions of social power.
City in the Old West.

One is named for a prize, and the other is named
for one of the cities in which the prize is given.

Object introduced into a place for purposes of
research or investigation. A long, slender tool.

Extinct animals,
animals prized for their fur,
swift creatures roaming the hills at night.

A city in Devonshire, on the English Channel,
known for a small Christian sect founded in
1830; an American breed of chicken with
gray and bluish-black striped feathers.

Cheap whiskey that comes in a green bottle.

Tiny Mediterranean principality known for its botanical gardens and roulette wheels.

Library

Born in Louisville, Baltimore, or New York City.
He was adopted in 1914 or '18 and, according to
different records, grew to the height of 5'3", 5'7",
or 5'10". His parents included a Methodist minister
and his wife, an obese woman relative, mother,
and grandmother. De Witt Clinton High School,
New York University, Harvard. Countee L. Porter.
Countee P. Cullen. Countee Cullen.

Apartment

According to Lincoln Steffens,
Mabel Dodge's apartment at 23 Fifth Avenue
was a place where
"Socialists,
Trade-Unionists,
Anarchists,
Suffragists,
Poets,
Relations,
Lawyers,
Murderers,
'Old Friends,'
Psychoanalysts,
I.W.W.'s,
Single Taxers,
Birth Controllers,
Newspapermen,
Artists,
Modern-Artists,
Clubwomen,
Woman's-place-is-in-the-home Women,
Clergymen,
and just plain men all met . . .
and stammering in an unaccustomed freedom a kind of speech called Free,
exchanged a variousness in vocabulary called,
in euphemistic optimism,
opinions."

After Emma Goldman

I want my sweetheart, Willie Boy.
I want to give him the treasure box.
She is simply starved
and will swallow him alive
when she gets hold of him.

The treasure box is full of red wine
and waits for Willie to drink it all.

I is hungry and thirsty.

You are like Anarchism to me.
The more I struggle for it
the further it moves away from me.

Let me forget that I have neither home nor country.

After Heinrich Heine

Things are worse in hell than our theater
managers know, otherwise they wouldn't put on
so many bad plays, in hell it is quite hellishly
hot, and when I was there during the dog days,
I found it unendurable. We get few official reports
from there. That the poor souls down there are
forced to spend all their time reading bad sermons
written up here; this is slander. It is not that awful in Hell;
Satan would never concoct such a subtle form of torture.
To me, Hell is a big kitchen with an endlessly long stove
on which stand three rows of iron pots.

From GIANT WALL (A Notebook)

A
new
planet
gleams
in
its
puddle
of
ink

Water
fills
the
basin
with
light
from
distant
stars

Angel Atrapado I

We did not know we could fall safely from there to here, from the sky's burgundy balcony, where we had been watching ourselves sleeping, to the cracked and tiled slabs on which we were walking. The name bolted to the side of the dented red car means either "star" or "it does not go."

We did not know we could move among the city's inhabitants as if they were letters of the world spelling themselves out, shifting particles and planes beneath clouds-filled skies. The downstairs neighbor came up and announced: "You must not throw ashes in my face when you go out at night and look for the moon."

The birds did not leave the city except when they rise and circle above its poured concrete towers, riding the currents twisting and untwisting above the heat. The roses are almost the same color as the zinnias in the painting above it, on the sunlit white wall facing the mountain. A little man with three identical heads stacked on top of each other. Books behind narrow wooden door. Across the street, a dog barks at the shadow inhabiting his favorite chair.

"This is the house of the Egyptian twins." Mountains benches, flowers. The preferred style for monuments is French, a language found in mostly high-priced restaurants near the museum. Brick ceiling above glass. Costumed waiters come with each marriage certificate.

It began: "They wanted a woman who could collar drunks with duller cranks." It ended: "We cooked some rumors, and began fanning the smoke across the river." The blue panels of Edificio Sucre against the sky, one orange letter rising above the roof. Thick black lines float between definitions, either a crooked row of cardinal numbers or caricatures from the Encyclopedia of Outdated Emotions.

The red and gold Persian carpet from California

You talked yourself into any knot but the one that let you breathe.

You orbited the earth, a yellow angel.

He returns to the village of arson, his eyes on fire.

Angel Atrapado IV

It was my body I was watching. I was both in it and constructing it, both in the pool of pleasure it was receiving and quietly building low sinuous walls to prevent its liquids from flowing away. I was a man or a woman or both. I was looking at it, walking toward it, was lying there waiting to be reached.

The scene was a movie or sentences resembling a movie, Isolated instances melting into each other when they were not. I was the camera or arrow (the eyes that see the scene but the body that is not in it) moving across the screen in front of me, making the details of what was taking place there assume a life of their own. And in their own life, these sentences became bodies moving about before me. I saw them, was them, but did not know whether the "I" that was seeing was mine or not.

The scene changed or became clearer, I couldn't decide. I saw this mute "I", it was a he. He was lying there. Another he (perhaps another me) was approaching. It was a surgeon, someone who could perform operations, could dissect a body into its different sentences, its separate lines of information. I couldn't tell if he was giving information to the one lying on the table or taking it away. I couldn't tell what I was being given to read.

It was the only way I could be there seeing this scene, as a picture looking down at a table, the body or book that used to be mine. Someone, perhaps you, gave it to me, and then took it away, giving me a book describing a body, giving me the outline of what I used to inhabit. I was what was missing from its pages, I was what was not being written there, a place emptied of all voices. The "I" that you crushed when it first cried out, the one trying now to speak to the body or book it once inhabited. The "I" was what was removed, the "I" now looking back at what is there.

Angel Atrapado VII

The one who says: I was almost alive or nearly dead or somewhere in between, a dirty flask full of secondhand tears. I thought I was inside this room inside myself, but I was walking past the window. I saw you listening to what was being said, examining the syllables, their cold sibilants, and then holding them up and asking what they were that you too could use them. But we hadn't yet spoken, nor (as it turned out) would we ever.

The one who says: They want to be friends but they cannot help themselves, and think it is business. Or they think they are moving towards business when they want to be friends. The one who licks his or her golden lips when you expose your neck, raises your head above the words you have been trained to follow all along.

The one who says: I grow inside you growing inside me, feel your voice inside the voice used to speak, the voice falling back into itself, the voice barely able to listen to itself listening, the voice full of borrowed words sent forth in borrowed clothes, the voice of that one over there lying under the bed, asking for something other than money but metallic nevertheless

The one who says: an imbecile and his rabbit huddle under a decrepit family tree. A coolie and a taxi dancer run past the underworld. A root and its patient argue over chess.

Or is it the one who says: I am watching bullet riddled bodies tumble beneath the final layers of evening's gift, their pastel colors describing a wall beyond the horizon, and what is taking place in front of me started burning through all pages held up to the light.

Or is it finally the voice cursing itself for having spoken at all, that one and that one and that one, all of them pushing toward the mouth or empty sky they once thought was theirs and theirs alone.

Self-Portrait with Max Beckmann

One vision alone would be much simpler
but then it would not exist

Love in an animal sense is an illness
I am not a squirrel

though I have been told I eat like one
Everywhere attempts are being made

to lower our capacity for happiness
to the level of termites

Have you not been with me
in the deep hollow of a champagne glass

where blue lobsters crawl around
waiters serving flaming hats

mounted with pink and yellow flowers
Have you not given up searching

for a way out of this phantom-plagued
machine
Have you not observed the Law of Surface

in the poisonous splendor of the orchid
Perhaps we will enjoy ourselves

in the forms we have been given
I am an acrobat climbing a ladder

A man in a tuxedo smoking a smelly cigar
The clothes are a disguise

To you, I am not a very nice man
who was lucky enough

to marry a beautiful woman from Graz
but to myself, I am a painter

who sleeps in a small room
adjacent to the corridors

of an endless mansion

Second Metabolic Isthmus Sestina

Fortune sex book always wants this
This fortune sex book always wants
Book always wants this fortune sex
Wants this fortune sex book always
Always want this sex fortune book
Sex book always wants this fortune

Sex butler always want this fortune
Fortune sex butler always wants this
Always wants this fortune sex butler
This fortune sex butler always wants
Wants this fortune sex butler always
Butler always wants this fortune sex

Butler knows aunt wants fortune sex
Sex butler knows aunt wants fortune
Aunt wants fortune sex butler knows
Fortune sex butler knows aunt wants
Wants aunt sex butler knows fortune
Know aunt wants fortune sex butler

Must mate this fortune sex butler
Butler must mate this fortune sex
This fortune sex butler must mate
Sex butler must mate this fortune
Fortune sex butler must mate this
Mate this fortune sex butler must

Sex mate butler last this must
Must mate sex butler last this
Butler this last must mate sex
This must mate sex butler last
Must sex butler last this mate

Last false sex butler must mate
Mate last false sex butler must
Sex butler must last mate false
Must mate sex last false butler
Butler must mate last false sex

Sex always wants book this fortune
Aunt fortune sex butler knows this book
Sex butler wants mate book last

Dunk Not in Europe

Day docks seared tongue under barn
Dazed and dyed night dunks its list
All stern sleeves are in—
Rock day shines a muddled shine
Under fine nights nick a house,
Tapped, tastes so much wetter,
Stool prey, fallen, leaves, dank—
With day locked, night bleaches and dunks—
All day veils and glance flutes
Dazed and dyed night dunks its list
Weariness is a dank sigh
Odor rats fold up the night

Section 3
(1996–2004)

Variations on a Sentence by Laura (Riding) Jackson

There is something to be told about us for the telling of which we all wait. Something to be told. There is something about the telling of which we all wait to be told. Something telling. About something which we all wait for the telling to be told. Something about the wait. The telling of something is there to be told. Something about us for the telling. We all wait for the something to be told. The telling is there for us. Something telling is to be told about us. The telling wait. The wait telling us to be told. The wait is something for all the telling. Something to be told about us which is for the telling. Something for us. Something for the wait. Something told for the telling. All we told is something about the us which is there. We wait to be told about the us which is telling something. All is there for the telling of which is there to be told. All is something to be told. All telling is something told about us for which we wait. All of something which we wait for. All telling told. All of us telling wait to be told something. There is the telling to be told. The something told, the something us, the something telling. Something tell is there. There telling us to be told something for which we wait. There is for the telling something of which we wait to be told. Something about us for the wait. Something about the telling to be told. To be something is to wait to be told. Is there something about us for which we wait? About telling us we all wait for something. The telling and the told, the we and us which wait. Us telling which wait is there to be told. Which telling is to be told. Told there is something about us. Told there is the wait. Told of the wait which is something about us. We all told about something. Which something about us for the telling? The us for which we wait. Which there is something we all wait for? Something of which we tell. There is the wait to be told, there is the telling about us. The told something, the telling there. For the wait, the telling us. For the told is for the telling. Wait for the telling to be told. Something for which we wait, the telling to be telling.

Russian Letter 1

It is said, the past
sticks to the present

like glue,
that we are flies

struggling to pull free
It is said, someone

cannot change
the clothes

In which
their soul

was born.
I, however,

would not
go so far

Nor am I Rembrandt,
master of the black

and green darkness
the hawk's plumes

as it shrieks
down from the sky

Russian Letter 3

Dear Painter of Clouds
What proof will there be

after the shopkeeper
sweeps our dust into the gutter

And yet these moments are not
anyone's banner, not something

to be waved in the wind
sent aloft

a kite in the shape of a fish
vigorous sail above a winter beach

where we sit and watch and walk
always back

to our separate rooms in the city
The fast full sky is not

where we are swimming
if we are swimming at all

Dear Syllables Retrieved from the Rain
Dear Wind Alone with Your Song

these fallen words are my ode
to you

Russian Letter 6

Amidst this haste and filth
besides the river's black violin

its sluggish summer tune
should I tell you how

you hide the dead
without singing

Dear Ungovernable Lament
Are you like a log

abandoned on a road of dead trees
Or is your life a stone

smashed to
bits

About the one of yourself
and the one of the one

that is not you
but is the memory of what you wanted

I have only this to say
How is your life with an image

or has your memory started fading
until what you can pry loose

from the sea
is an island

etched in blue smoke
Dear Steam

How is your life with a stranger
from this world

the one we once walked in
argued over

tried to burn

Postcard from Trakl

Memory's branch quivers
beneath the weight of a butterfly

How am I to know what it wants
without asking

Could it be that simple, the question
and then the answer

Why do we fall outside of these additions
or consult the zodiac surrounding us

read its rotten walls ad bulb glare
Why substitute names for things

when the things name us
(our vowels and consonants)

into their sleep,
one from which we will never awaken

Am I just an echo drifting back to myself
who is sitting beneath the river

drinking air
Something must have told me to say this

a rock or the memory of a rock
falling toward the shadow it once owned

830 Fireplace Road

(Variations on a sentence by Jackson Pollock)

"When I am in my painting, I'm not aware of what I'm doing."

When aware of what I am in my painting, I'm not aware.

When I am my painting, I'm not aware of what I am.

When what, what when, what of, when in, I'm not painting my I.

When painting, I am in what I'm doing, not doing what I am,

When doing what I am, I'm not in my painting.

When I am of my painting, I'm not aware of when, of what,

of what I'm doing, I am not aware, I'm painting,

of what, when, my, I, painting, in painting,

when of, of what, in when, in what painting

not aware, not in, not of, not doing, I'm in my I

in my am, not am in my, not of when I am, of what,

painting "what" when I am, of when I am, doing, painting.

When painting, I'm not doing. I am in my doing. I am painting.

Borrowed Love Poems

1.

What can I do, I have dreamed of you so much
What can I do, lost as I am in the sky

What can I do, now that all
the doors and windows are open

I will whisper this in your ear
as if it were a rough draft

something I scribbled on a napkin
I have dreamed of you so much

there is no time left to write
no time left on the sundial

for my shadow to fall back to earth
lost as I am in the sky

2.

What can I do, all the years that we talked
and I was afraid to want more

What can I do, now that these hours
belong to neither you nor me

Lost as I am in the sky
what can I do, now that I cannot find

the words I need
when your hair is mine

now that there is no time to sleep
now that your name is not enough

3.

What can I do, if a red meteor wakes the earth
and the color of robbery is in the air

Now that I dream of you so much
my lips are like clouds

drifting above the shadow of one who is asleep
Now that the moon is enthralled with a wall

What can I do, if one of us is lying on the earth
and the other is lost in the sky

4.

What can I do, lost as I am in the wind
and lightning that surrounds you

What can I do, now that my tears
are rising toward the sky

only to fall back
into the sea again

What can I do, now that this page is wet
now that this pen is empty

5.

What can I do, now that the sky
has shut its iron door

and bolted clouds
to the back of the moon

now that the wind
has diverted the ocean's attention

now that a red meteor
has plunged into the lake

now that I am awake
now that you have closed the book

6.

Now that the sky is green
and the air is red with rain

I never stood in
the shadow of pyramids

I never walked from village to village
in search of fragments

that had fallen to earth in another age
What can I do, now that we have collided

on a cloudless night
and sparks rise

from the bottom of a thousand lakes

7.

To some, the winter sky is a blue peach
teeming with worms

and the clouds are growing thick
with sour milk

What can I do, now that the fat black sea
is seething

now that I have refused to return
my borrowed dust to the butterflies

their wings full of yellow flour

8.

What can I do, I never believed happiness
could be premeditated

What can I do, having argued with the obedient world
that language will infiltrate its walls

What can I do, now that I have sent you
a necklace of dead dried bees

and now that I want to
be like the necklace

and turn flowers into red candles
pouring from the sun

9.

What can I do, now that I have spent my life
studying the physics of good-bye

every velocity and particle in all the waves
undulating through the relapse of a moment's fission

now that I must surrender this violin
to the sea's foaming black tongue

now that January is almost here
and I have started celebrating a completely different life

10.

Now that the seven wonders of the night
have been stolen by history

Now that the sky is lost and the stars
have slipped into a book

Now that the moon is boiling
like the blood where it swims

Now that there are no blossoms left
to glue to the sky

What can I do, I who never invented
anything

and who dreamed of you so much
I was amazed to discover

the claw marks of those
who preceded us across this burning floor

Ing Grish

"You need to speak Singlish to express a Singaporean feeling."
—Catherine Liu

I never learned Singlish.

I cannot speak Taglish, but I have registered
the tonal shifts of Dumglish, Bumglish, and Scumglish.

I do not know Ing Grish, but I will study it down to its
black and broken bones.

I do not know Ing Gwish, but I speak dung and dungaree,
satrap and claptrap.

Today I speak barbecue and canoe.

Today I speak running dog and yellow dog.

I do not know Spin Gloss, but I hear humdrum and humdinger,
bugaboo and jigaboo.

I do not know Ang Grish, but I can tell you that my last name
consists of three letters, and that technically all of them are vowels.

I do not know Um Glish, but I do know how to eat with two sticks.

O but I do know English because my father's mother was English
and because my father was born in New York in 1921
and was able to return to America in 1949
and become a citizen

I no speak Chinee, Chanel, or Cheyenne.

I do know English because I am able to tell others
that I am not who they think I am.

I do not know Chinese because my mother said that I refused to learn it
from the moment I was born, and that my refusal
was one of the greatest sorrows of her life,
the other being the birth of my brother.

I do know Chinese because I understood what my mother's friend told her
one Sunday morning, shortly after she sat down for tea:
"I hope you don't mind that I parked my helicopter on your roof."

Because I do not know Chinese, I have been told that means
I am not Chinese by a man who translates from the Spanish.
He said that he had studied Chinese and was therefore closer
to being Chinese than I could ever be. No one publicly disagreed with him,
which, according to the rules of English, means he is right.

I do know English and I know that knowing it means
that I don't always believe it.

The fact that I disagree with the man who translates from the Spanish
is further proof that I am not Chinese because all the Chinese
living in America are hardworking and earnest
and would never disagree with someone who is right.
This proves I even know how to behave in English.

I do not know English because I got divorced and therefore
I must have misunderstood the vows I made at City Hall.

I do know English because the second time I made a marriage vow
I had to repeat it in Hebrew.

I do know English because I know what "fortune cookie" means
when it is said of a Chinese woman.

An authority on poetry announced that I discovered that I was Chinese
when it was to my advantage to do so.

My father was afraid that if I did not speak English properly
I would be condemned to work as a waiter in a Chinese restaurant.

My mother, however, said that this was impossible because
I didn't speak Cantonese, because the only language
waiters in Chinese restaurants know how to speak was Cantonese,
which she did not consider Chinese.

I do not speak either Cantonese or English, Ang Glish or Ing Grish.

Anguish is a language everyone can speak, but no one listens to it.

I do know English because my father's mother was Ivy Hillier.
She was born and died in Liverpool, after living in America and China,
and claimed to be a descendant of the Huguenots.

I do not know English because I misheard my grandmother and thought
she said that I was a descendant of the Argonauts.

I do know English because I remember what "Made in Japan" meant
when I was a child.

I learn over and over again that I do not know Chinese.

Yesterday a man asked me how to spell my last name in English,
because he was sure that I had been mispronouncing it
and that if this was how my father pronounced it,
then the poor man had been wrong all his life.

I do not know Chinese even though my parents conversed in it every day.

I do know English because I had to ask the nurses
not to put my muttering mother in a straitjacket,
and reassure them that I would be willing to stay with her
until the doctor made his rounds the following morning.

I do know English because I left the room when the doctor told me
I had no business being there.

I do not know Chinese because during the Vietnam War
I was called a gook instead of a chink and realized
that I had managed to change my spots without meaning to.

I do not know English because when father said that he would
like to see me dead, I was never sure quite what he meant.

I do not know Chinese because I never slept with a woman
whose vagina slanted like my mother's eyes.

I do not know either English or Chinese and, because of that,
I did not put a gravestone at the head of my parents' graves
as I felt no language mirrored the ones they spoke.

the late tale

then several (like five) venture there
(site: transparent teal blue plane)
maybe meet several (like nine) more
then several (more like ten)
gather their flesh outside
(nerve directions: encase)
erect spines near several others
then several (imagine eleven)
see several others being erect (maybe noble)
then five (guessing seven) chatter
opposite downtrodden eight (maybe less)
then maybe less help maybe more
duel several others (maybe even more)
then the then dwindles beside the the
leaving even less gathered
none erect
then the superbly sculpted supine figures
(imagine neat pile)
are raised open-mouthed because haunted
then the several open-mouthed
haunted figures venture
near quiet abodes
(they penetrate cement castles, insect domiciles)
then several armed (some men)
dangle red celery before children
dressed like donkeys (possible sacrifice)
then the donkeys (maybe they are children)
shed their purple capes

before fleeing their haunted parents
then more meet less even then the less faces more
then the darkness itself
releasing molten green cascades
fiery tongues descend
demanding more donkeys
then the donkeys aren't children anymore
because different celestial effects
infect their heads
then the dreamers
(imagine one maybe three)
tell their tale near the fire
then the tale (maybe more)
explodes above the telling
then the donkeys
(are they haunted children?)
slide like stale bubbled cream
inside the children
their red smiles
then the disguised children descend
demanding larger purple capes
then several more stories are recited beside the fire
then these stories
botched exhumations
extinguishing the stories before them
(note: noises [notes]
begin breaking
ice-clogged lake,
teal green plane)
because each tries extinguishing the others
their frozen syllables dissolve
more tales

(are they holes?
are they moles?)
emerge
then several marriages break
leaving the children wandering
then the wandering comets
(imagine children) return
their blue stones exciting
the Cimmerian darkness
then several figures
(some are comets,
others are children)
converge inside the wooden abode
(termite-eaten table?)
rotted cellar beams?
master's teak-lined bedroom?
where the dreamer
leaves the dream
others seek
believing therein lies the answer
forgetting they have the lake
the ice
the comet
the red stone
then the answer becomes the little haunted question
(imagine comet)
suspended above lacustrine drinker
(green marble statue)
then once more the then
begins breaking factories
little sweatshops crammed together
under fiery planets

the children swear opposite the donkeys
the donkeys are secretly infidels
disguised hermits
large drudge machines
they (donkeys, perhaps children) become heroes
when they reduce their drivel quotient
then the children hidden inside the donkeys
begin exhausting their parents
several disinherit their progeny
others take downhearted hikes
then the ice age begins once more
(maybe twice)
then the children are cooled inside the frozen lake machine
the parents become delirious
(huge venomous parties)
the donkeys are freed
everyone rejoices
then the donkeys make their mistake
they dance beside the fire
then several (maybe more) meet several others
(some venture where there
they once gathered erect)
then the celestial delivery systems begin their bombardment
then the here (imagine infinite more) empties itself
before the darkness becomes the emblazoned shield
whose foretelling occurred
(inside the faded flame once called time)
when the tale began loosening the blackened tiles
lodged inside the infinitely broken sea

Nasty Orders Pacifies Queen

Antonia greases limp braids
Billy humps mezzanine contraband
Criticism interrupts nozzle deadline
Depression jargon opens evening
Event kickoff parade forecast
Flounder lord quashes goblet
Gashes Merlin's reflective ham
Horace neutralizes serious incident
Itinerant orators trounce jinx
Juvenile peccadilloes urbane kennel
Kiosk quip vapors legible
Livid research wanderer masticates
Meteor shower xenophobes nullify
Neckline tempo yearning ossification
Office undergoes zephyr plague
Punitive vexations anchor quill
Querulous woodwind buccaneer recital
Renounce xeroxing cheery swigs
Salami yams dill tuna
Turtle zebra eagle unicorn
Uhlan admonishes fulminating veil
Vertiginous blue gladiator wall
Windward caravel hinders xebec
Xylophone duress initiates yank
Yurt exquisite joss ziggurat
Zeppelin flames kindle Antonia

Peter Lorre Reminisces About Being a Sidekick

Iron cloud, bronzed sunset, stolen scream:
I wasn't always a feverish lepidopterist
chasing whistling chariots in a stadium.
My wax lacked coherence; my human hairs glistened.
Perhaps you would like to come in off the ledge
and share a mug of hot cocoa laced with absinthe.
Or is that the kind of little naughtiness you prefer to shun?
Have you noticed there's lots of snow
Clinging to my last Fabergé egg?
Take off your tie, throw away your shoes.
Have you seen my collection of portholes,
some pried from the very finest luxury liners
to have foundered on these rocks?
It's not that I am given to issuing a high-resolution
lightly thawed whoop or two
whenever my oversized eyelids
belly fat knuckles start twittering
and the crease in my gabardines start gabbing
to the pleats gathered at the corner, waiting
for the light to change its spots,
but I just love yodeling,
"O sweet spotless tyrannosaurus,
why hast thou handcuffed me
to the Hunting Lodge of Unrepentant Nations
and their sprawling kin? Am I not
allowed a few extra paces
before I am commanded
to run into the woods?"

Such timely intermissions prove
how newly minted and hot I became,
while sitting on a painted horse,
surrounded by dancing dandelions.
Did I forget to mention the adventures of Smoky Muskrat,
Maison Spittle, and Cheap Varmint Night and his Band,
the Sheep Bladder Brigade? Or am I being too allegorical,
too much a one-night pill flipper in a copycat's storm?
Will I ever be regarded as truly satisfying?
Can I become one who exudes
a heroic magnetic profile?
Become one whose blessed visage pulls the dust
off your brow of well-endowed verbs?
Will you remember me as something more
than an imported bandana
when I am draped in bad blood squirted from a can
made of recycled helmets retired ogres pitched in a ditch?
Hey, are you glugging to the ghosts of Salvation Coliseum?
This isn't a resurrection factory, you simian of slime.
What are you doing? Walking your toast
down to the coroner's barn? Quit hawking
your perforated hanky, there is always more of this
where this came from. Remember, the last time
you had your brain amputated, you were required
to sacrifice your definitions of meandering reincarnations
in favor of a satchel of bologna pizzas.
Or were just another hunger artist
quick to lick the trumpet of integrity?
Hard to dream about the outside when it stops
raining long enough to forget you once had
a memorable name. This is where I get off
the bus, buster. Or is it Bruiser or Boozer,

Flappy or Winsome with an axe?
On the other side of the lake lives a two-headed dragon.
Pink smoke rises from the nostrils of one known
as Ying, while blue tears fall from the one known as Yank.
It is rumored that they used to be Siamese twins
but got tired of eating from the same Hollywood bowl.
As a dishwasher, I became familiar with their plight,
and tried to comfort them, but with little consequence.
You encounter all sorts of shadows in the game preserve.
Some have been suspended in the trees for eons,
their souls locked inside the recyclable peanut
butter jars insulating the wizard's hexagonal library.
That's how I plan to get promoted to Senior Gatekeeper.
A small wagon floated downstream, guided by nymphs.
Huge fragrant bouquets descended from the rafters,
quickly covering the stage, but, by then,
the headline star had fled into the closet
the management rented out for such occasions.
Time to hoist your mortal spoils out of bed, Bunky.
I wasn't trying to become you when the mountain
tugged itself together, collapsing outside the doghouse
where I pass my afternoons, dreaming of the day
my portrait will finally hang in the dog museum.
You pass more than afternoons, you blasphemous pustule
on the noble edifices that have been studiously
erected by the fleet of robots, sleek and newly released,
like a certain frog's vivacious belch, from
the recently upgraded prison recreation facility
just down the road from the gas station where I saw you
licking grease off the monkey they keep
tucked behind the cash register.
I wasn't always this gentle. In fact,

I wasn't always an Austro-Hungarian umpire, either.
Twice I have been somewhere
outside your sovereignty. Once I was even Japanese,
but that was before the war brought us home,
to the blue picket fence draped with ribbons and razors.
Quit smooching in the mirror, goggle eyes. You got a face
that could pass as a kangaroo's pouch.
Not that I don't muster up some small careful affection
for that doomed race of puddle hoppers,
but we all jump into oblivion, don't we?
Maybe you ought to get into another lie of work.
Maybe you ought to fold your name somewhere else,
sign on someone else's dotted line
since you were never issued one in the first place.
I am sure I can find you an envelope big enough.
What about the barrel of forks you hid in the alley?
Say, what are you doing here anyway?
Who said you could stop by and smear lemongrass
meringue over your cloudy lapels? You think
you got something big to say? Something momentous.
Or is it that you had to memorize how to be agreeably silent
in order to escape the men with lightning in their eyes?

Domestic Bliss

If I am as cute as a button
why have you spent the past hour
hunting for the one that rolled down your sleeve

onto the aluminum siding bus
carrying rows of disillusioned tourists
toward the chimney heart of our once famous city

Didn't you say that you didn't like that coat
that the buttons were too big for someone
possessing your delicate bone structure

Why isn't there more meat on this chicken.
It's as if the damned thing began starving itself
once it knew what the future had in store for it.

Is this what they mean by "organic"
I agree. We don't need to go on
fighting like this. We could learn

another way to fight, one that wouldn't
expend so many baccalaureates of bituminous energy
Perhaps a nap from which we would wake up

refreshed as a fish dropped back into a forest pond
Okay, platinum mousetrap of a higher celestial order
one of us would whisper to the other

you get on your side of the rubber volcano
and I'll get on mine. But before you do
would you mind mending my hind paws

I need to get that sand back into my open veins

In Between and Around

And all the while we were kissing,
the two of us, and the many we are,
were standing, kneeling, or spinning
upside down in the long arms of prayer,
waiting to be kissed.
Pimply slumps of pockmarked muscles.
Closet behind schoolyard
back-alley train station
midnight morning
lifts through blue light
locked inside eyes and breath
held in wet palms.
Hands and mouth gripping.
All paws and fur.
Tepid tongue, slippery teeth.
First joyful snake stabs.
All the while we were kissing
on a dusty summer afternoon,
someone was standing outside us,
watching our shadows perpetrate a body
on soft asphalt beneath cloudless sky.
Walking, as if there is somewhere to go.
Petulant scowl, lips that flower,
Scorched red petals swelling
neither to be caressed nor plucked.
Waiting all the while for the ones
inside us who are kissing
to see the ones who are,

behind and before
the ones without boundaries
and the places opening within.
The ones pushing and pushing
against words and air
and the beams of light lodged between them,
as if the doors would open
and the form presently inhabited
would be released into a dimension
from which there is no return,
particles and wavelengths
flowing through each other.
One of them thinking, always afraid
to fill a thought with words, breathe
outside the boundaries of the third person,
though eyes in hazy half-light
watch the lips parting with each breath,
and the body beside the one
who is sleeping sweats.
The sweat rolling down the face
mingles with tears, and the tears
moisten the lips. The lips of the one
who wished and waited and finally spoke
or the lips of the one who wouldn't and didn't.
Rows of mouths, closed or twisted,
Open or shut in dunes and curtains
Flowering under the monument's hammer.
Of these tears and the tears beside them,
the ones about which you cannot speak
and are afraid to see, of these and others
the *Book of Trembling* is written.
Flailing hands, unraveling hair.

Hands sliding around each other
like scarves unable to form a knot
or a knot unable to be loosened.
A pond flecked with summer's last daubs.
And the body ones sees beneath
and within the fabric rustling
and shifting with every breath
drawn across taut sweep of skin,
eyes fixated, air held in lungs,
smoldering there, the sounds
swelling louder and louder
than the thoughts releasing them.
All while voices are rising
towards one's mouth, borrowed, broke
or temporarily possessed, two tremulous
ropes are kissing behind and beyond
the ones who are crawling, shifting
away from and towards,
near and under and beside
this around nearing and nearer.
Sometimes a pleasant wriggling gasps.
A sigh like that of one in pain.
And all the while the ones
we imagine ourselves to be
go on kissing and kissing,
hands prying apart,
fingers squeezing
twisting hard buttons,
plucking at metal and cloth,
and the rippling overlap of two
consecutive, stretching, pushing forms
located on the physical plane

between liquid and solid disintegrates
the dorsal trajectories,
as they go on,
as if that is all they can do,
the only place of sustenance
bring where their mouths mesh,
all they want being the mouth
opening and closing around, over, and between.
And the kissing goes on
even when the body grows lax,
soft and malleable as a spoon of lead and wax,
something to thud against the wind.
And the wind moves aside,
as the kissing continues,
and the mouths move aside,
as the bodies become plants
on the ocean floor, spinning within
the motions of air's sweet tremors.
And the kissing begins to take hold,
while inside the ones who are kissing,
the ones whose mouths have merged
into a single speaker of divided thoughts,
are other mouths, hands, feet.
And their voices begin rising, expanding,
and there is no end to the clamoring, whispers,
whistles, mumbles, and screams,
while the ones who are kissing go on
because there is nothing and nowhere else,
no other hospital but here
where lips are meeting.
Shoulders, arms, fingers, eyelids,
and elbows join with feet, ribcage, and legs,

mouths open, words or sounds
resembling words emerge
and melt among sounds of cars honking,
curses of the hurt and shunned,
tremors of astronauts dreaming,
sunlight drifting across shutters.
And the sounds of the kissing
reach the ones lined up inside
waiting to be kissed.
Some feel a mouth or mouths,
and others don't,
while the shadows
in the hallways their bodies form
keep kissing, lips
pressing and pushing against lips,
teeth and tongue.
And sometimes a voice tells them
they are the silhouettes of the ones
waiting, wanting, refusing, afraid
of the kissing that goes on and on,
and the kissing that brings
something more, something else,
the kissing that is just
a sign of what will happen,
a taste or touch.
Murmurs leading to tremors
and more kissing
piled on top of the kisses.
Having watched, having seen.
After before and during a kiss
that never begins.
And this voice whispers

about the taste or touch
that some mouths never know
and about which they cannot speak,
having never tasted or been tasted.
The one tied to the chair obtained by the family.
The one strapped in the chair provided by the state.
And all that they have to say about kissing
That has never been heard by those who have kissed,
And the ones trying not to hear what all the ones
Inside them are saying,
Thought bending to mouth
Whose mouth is being met now.
All the while.

Conversation after Midnight

The civilization of green ants
met last work or month
(Your sense of time a concept
I don't yet understand
and besides I wasn't there)
and they elected me to come here,
even though me was still not me or even an I,
an unarticulated murmur, maybe that,
at best some dust of unlikely possibility,
I was nevertheless elected to be
among you, to arrive and to periodically whimper,
howl stir scream cry
in a black spring night
gone sour with the images of the moon
(O oarless alabaster boat)
(O pearly O sitting high above the savannah)
So many poets still call on,
As if it's the nearest neighbor,
a ubiquitous presence signifying
the right proportion of magic and tragedy
when they want to let everyone know
how divine they have become in the interim
kissed by capital G you might say
but I need not tell you that you are hardly divine
a lump is more like it if it is what you are
My name is Cerise Tzara Aschheim Yau
I am your child
I have been here a little over a month

crying shitting eating sleepless restless
as I extend my arms and kick my feet
And I can see that you are perplexed by what
I am trying to tell you through the infant
you hold in your hands, the one you
think of as your child,
which is true, but I too am your child,
I who am an I, you, me, two, three,
the one elected by the green ants and the dolphins
their leader whispered something
(Was I to repeat it word-for-word
as if such repetition is accurate
a higher form of mimesis than trompe l'oeil?)
something I have forgotten during
the during and enduring from the to the,
here and there not yet having hardwired
their coordinates within the celestial tumult
something in words about and through them perhaps
I can't remember which is why no amount of
beseeching is going to yield anything more from me
than I am the poem, yes I am the one
you want to write or be written by in this time
you boob or should I say *Boobus Sanctimonius*
I am the poem
you need to write to and for
the one that isn't the one or one
but one of the ones who might
step out of the flickering skyline of transparent shadows
and say to you years from now
hey old farting sag face
dim bulb in a dark and gloomy night
why did you spend years and years

shitting all that goop on to pristine white page
after white page
and you will smile
knowing I know I know the answer
knew it before here became
the time-space continuum
I inhabit
but this is a conversation that will unfold
at and in another time right now being
right now I am hungry
so go get me something warm to drink
will you Bud
And hey mister whoever you are
you better quit
calling me
Pipalotti Poopsalot
Starvin' Marvin and Kid
I gotta name
why doncha use it

Broken Sonnet

The world weeps. There are no tears
To be found. It is deemed a miracle.
The President appears on screens
In Villages and towns, in cities, in jungles
And jungles still affectionately called cities.
He appears on screens and reads a story.
Whose story is he reading and why?
What lessons are to be learned from this story
About a time that has not arrived, will not arrive, is here?
Time of fire and images of fire climbing a ladder to the sun.
Time of precious and semiprecious liquids.
Time of a man and a woman doused in ink
Rolling across streams and down valleys
Trying to leave some string of words behind.

In the Kingdom of Poetry

(after Carlos Drummond de Andrade)

Don't write poems
about yourself.

Don't call attention
to your revelations

or make confessions
even if your intention

is to expiate pain,
overcome guilt,

temper your
understandable anger.

Don't excavate
your mother's grief

brother's sexual torment
sister's thievery,

father's self-hatred
step-parent's fortuitous star chart.

Feelings are not poems.
Relatives should be left

where they are found
in the gutter

or by a cash register.
Don't write poems

about others.
Leave out husbands,

divorcees, alcoholics,
pimply adolescents and nurses.

There is already a surplus
of bad movie scripts.

Forget about friends
and enemies,

anniversaries
and special moments.

Someone in the greeting card business
has already covered these topics.

Don't write about
what is happening in the world,

the missing child
and the human remains,

the burning beach
and the swallowed page,

the president's
fiftieth speech.

Whatever happened there
isn't a poem.

Don't try and prove
how sensitive you are.

Others have already
claimed to be plants.

It isn't necessary to demonstrate
how insensitive you are

as this is already
an indisputable fact.

Don't write poems
linking

an ordinary event
in your life

—shaving, adjusting your bra, riding subway
admiring especially picturesque sunset—

to a significant moment in history
—pogrom, starvation, exile, assassination—

or to a myth—rape, jealousy, or rejection—
in fact to anything that has a theme.

Poems are not papers
delivered at conferences.

Don't sing about the joys of the city
or list the virtues of rural life.

Don't mention swans,
baloney, eyeball dryness,

or one-eared philosophers.
Picnics and paintings are not poems.

Don't resort to drama
or telling lies.

Don't use your yearning
as a starting point.

Secrets should be left
where they are.

Don't stand up
in a burning theater

And announce,
"no one listens to poetry."

Don't write poems
about poets

being underpaid.
Throw away

your memories,
bury your mirrors.

Section 4
(2005–2012)

Andalusia (1)

Time quietly peers in each window
but only the children find it funny

The second necklace we wear is the horizon
circling our waist and throats as the flowers
splash the sky with twilight and constellations
map out the mishap settling above the city

Abracadabras and horoscopes are impatient
with sleep and calligraphy

Grant me a sheet of paper that will not turn to ash
and this hand will write down afternoon's clouds
while you are hidden in my eyes, it is enough
this sheet of paper where I have hidden you
in these days of smoke and candle flames

Grant me time to pause and inquire of the clouds
if they have concealed you in their tears
behind a red sky in which the moon briefly flies

Grant me a sheet of paper that we might
live near the heat we once made when our hands
pelted the sky with ink and paint

Margins of thought curled like eyelashes
ask them if they remember us now
that our names are forgotten

Andalusia (2)

Rooftop roosters announce a new regime
Even at night, guided by the moon,

the sky can never find a cloud that fits
But, for the painter, each cloud is snug

Still, it is the sheet of paper that I want
and the ink that can keep these lovers safe

in the small garden where a lone bird
has stopped to look at its reflections

Andalusia (6)

Above against below beside near and around
Outside buttressed by imaginary flowers
Within a storm of letters echoing arches
Beneath a serpentine cloud dipped in red ink
Near a circle of lilies, each steeped petal
Beside twin strands of hexagonal tears
Above a shadow tracing its shadow

Andalusia (8)

I offer no proof that we were here
in sky's tent beneath sky's arrows

written in invisible ink on smoke
rising above the night we were together

I offer no proof that we were ever here
rolled together in a cloud's folds

now that it is an exquisite picture
that anyone can visit

Ill-Advised Love Poem

Come live with me
We could plant acorns

in each other's mouth
It would be our way

of greeting the earth
before it shoves us

back into the snow
our interior cavities

brimming with
disagreeable substances

Come live with me
before winter stops

to use the only pillow
the sky ever sleeps on

our interior cavities
brimming with snow

Come live with me
before spring

swallows the air

One Hundred Poems

Mercury
The Messenger is also known as Hydra, the many-headed monster with a poisonous dog's body; and each head multiplies every time someone lops it off.

Labyrinth
I can't remember why I was put here in the first place.

Universal
There is something in it for everyone.

First Prose Poem
In 1456, Bartolomeo Fazio described Jan van Eyck's *mappa mundi* as the most perfect work of its time, and that it's bird's eye view was from a higher vantage point than any bird could fly.

Biography of Li Po and Tu Fu
They were intoxicated with everything but themselves.

What Became of Me
A piece of smelly meat limping up and down stairs.

Warning Sign
Please do not remove any more dust from the moon.

All Eyes Were On X
There is no known cure for this.

What Did We Learn

A few things that helped some of us stay here a little longer.

Numerology

True love meets its perfect partner.

Fortune

You got to be kidding me.

Mr. Flummox Addresses the Assembly

I have a good mind, but I won't waste it on you

Dear Jetsam and Flotsam, Snoozy and Woozy

Greetings from the Terminal of Wounded Shepherds

Note on the Proper Preparation of "Supreme Surprise"

Until recently, there was no known substitute for "elephant drool."

The Most Important Rule Regarding Rodent Regalia

There should be nothing that is gray or brown, and this includes epaulets, buttons and tassels.

Slow Dance

Either the "Brooklyn Eyelid Sag" or "Death Becomes You. "

Tall Red Urn in the Shape of a Skyscraper

Voted most efficient storage unit for the moon's ashes.

Curious

What makes you want to wag your tail?

The Glass Eye on the Mantelpiece

The family gathers at noon, and waits for it to blink once more.

Exhortation

Please use our toilet paper the next time you visit.

Writing Machine

Made of silver threads and leather, this artificial hand once belonged to a poet.

Time Flies

When you remember to bring your wings to the swap meet.

I Can't Tell You How Happy I Am to Be Here

In accordance with the author's wishes, this space has been left blank.

Fairy Tale

Just married, a bride and groom enter a dark forest, never to be seen or heard from again.

Fairy Tale (2)

A horse whistles sharply, and its master comes running, carrying a silver tray.

Tropical Postcard

A black-and-white kitten climbs through a fence with a lizard's tail dangling from its mouth.

Familiar Complaint

My egg rolls look like dirty tube socks

Arrangement and Rearrangement
Love, Jetsam and Woozy, Flotsam and Snoozy

Zeus and Juno
A species that is able to successfully disguise itself.

Client
A person becomes convinced that you possess an arcane body of knowledge.

Scarecrows, Hedgerows, and Hedgehogs
Sleep will punish those you fail to rescue.

Store Motto
No more muss or fuss
When you bring us
Your broken blunderbuss

Paradiso Diaspora
Silent inlets

Credit
If you must know, the cars rusting in the yard are amulets.

The Eighth Dwarf
Doozy (aka Woozy) was last seen heading south on Interstate 74.

Sign
No matter what else you do, please remember to wash your hands before leaving tonight's performance.

Act Three
The light didn't go out at the last moment, you did.

Advertisement
Office desk kept in cloud suitcase.

A Pack of Barking Dogs
The image of you that you know best is waiting for another touch-up.

Blood Bank
"I am a magnet for mosquitoes."

Crime Scene
Dough nut, donut, do not, dew knot.

Indispensable
We have made available all kinds of products for people of small accomplishment.

Sage
Sometimes a wise man, other times a shrub with purple and white flowers, used in cooking.

Disaster
The tip of the iceberg is missing.

Complaint
I can't complain.

Danger, The Hotel Swimming Pool
Is full of all kinds of belly-fish.

Dessert precedes Disease
Spotted dick.

Dogs Do
Dog doo.

Sex Doll/Doll Sex
I am a full-service cervix waiting to service you.

Familiar Undiscovered Territory
There isn't anything else like it.

Anonymous and Particular
What we are in the face of time.

Newest Anagram Spy Camera
Snoop Spoon

Crime Scene
Is this *is* his or not

What Didn't We Learn
A few things that can help some of us stay here a little longer

Variation on Earlier Poem
I spotted Dick carrying a plate of spotted dick.

Bruised Feelings
Sour flower as sore eros rose

Proper Names
Abba and Baboo

Displayed at the Entrance to the Pavilion of Abject Objects
A Cemetery Guardhouse

Lovers

More, more, mi amore, and never ever stop to keep score

Dime Store Romance

He paid and stayed, while he played and played

Concert

Rapped, wrapped, rapt

Dilemma

Do you swear to tell the whole truth filled with nothing but lies.

Haiku (1)

Clomp, clomp, stump, clump, knock
Fiddle meddle in muddle
slam, clump, stump, stomp, stomp,

Haiku (2)

Red, yellow, and blue
Orange, eggplant, Granny Smith
Vermilion chartreuse

Biography

After X became Y, the name was entered into a registry, which was lost in the San Francisco Earthquake.

Do Me a Favor

Change the color of your thoughts before they become inflamed,
and you volunteer to clomp south toward the fiery polar caps.

Beside the Remains of a Pumice Tower

Scarlet moss, but never a flower

A Fleet of Droll Skeletons Out for a Stroll
Our intelligence still marinating in a wooden bowl

Rodents begin to look quite incredible
When they are no longer edible

I must decline your offer of leeks and lemur
I don't eat food cooked in an aluminum steamer.

Heaven's Carcass Flung Down from The Temple
How shall I write up this latest example?

Question
Who's going next said no one in particular to someone special?

Question (2)
Is she approaching or melting away?

Question (3)
Is this not the place where each of them is not seeing any other self instead of you and I?

Question (4)
Are being two things the same as believing you are feeling something inside?

Riddle
What do you ask of a frog that sticks its tongue out at you?

Announcement
Someone with the same name will give my lecture

Graffiti Blues
O Bliss, why are you smiling
when it's you I'll soon be defiling?

The Other Shoe
You can't decide how to practice waiting for this.

Don't Have a Fit
When real love doesn't fit you like a glove

Company Motto
This year's bonus
is next year's onus

Unspeakable Gifts
She did not anticipate that her anticipation would take such a drastic and monstrous form.

O My Little Worry Bead
Where will all my counting take me, if not that much closer to infinity?

Portrait
They were just doing this thing called kissing

Once You Hang Your Trash Out to Dry
Can you turn around, go home, and forget how to sigh?

Mr. Flummox Begins His Lecture
In this poem, I do not rhyme "chance" and "dance," nor do I use the words, "last, lest, or lust."

Jailhouse Fairytale

Once upon a time, a broken down drunk met a skunk in a real stinker

Chorus

I didn't know that I didn't know.

Familiar Family Fare

They were telling her what she was feeling, but she wasn't there.

Fairytale

The oldest elf was no longer growing old

Exclusive

I would like to inform you that my client expects some other pronouns to become available at your earliest convenience.

Vermilion

It is sometimes necessary to adjust the mixture of dragon's blood and elephant's blood when they are fighting each other.

Foundation

Flake white, shell white, silver white, Venetian white

I Was Born in Hell's Kitchen

And I never did leave.

Testimony

He did all that, but that was not all that he did.

Old Man

My white hair touches the moon, but no one notices.

Old Woman
I can't stomach the sounds of spring.

Guest of Honor
Monsieur Crocodile grins and grins
While his frightened host begins
Detailing his many, many sins

Marginalia
Escapade, Escalate, Escalator

My Name is Icarus
I once flew too close to you to learn your name

The World Is Our Oyster
Rotting in the sun.

Section 5
(2013–2020)

From My Adventures in Monochrome

1)

My fundamental self is at war with my multiple personalities
I love everything that does not belong to me, which is to say my life

but I despise everything that belongs to me:
education, inherited psychology, physical attributes.

In short, anything that is me because of exterior circumstances
My multiple selves are at war with my fundamental personality

Because one is never only one. I am aware that in writing this
I have committed an error of diplomacy

I recognize that people will claim these notes and thoughts are confused,
poorly expressed (as if expression has anything to do with it), emphatic,

for they have been written day by day,
even during the rain that threatens to close down the sky

I know that many will regard these statements
as another example of bad taste

a poor substitute for poetry
when in fact poetry is not what I am after

My fundamental self despises all that belongs to me:
multiples personalities, butterflies, and silent hoarding

Each more poorly expressed than the previous error of diplomacy
Who claims these notes are inherited circumstances

My multiple selves are at war with substitutes for poetry
My fundamental self is at war with poems offered as substitutes

I know that many will conclude these statements do not belong to me
I am aware in writing this during the rain that it is not raining

3)

I recently
declared
that the
artist of tomorrow
will continuously
recreate herself
by being able
to levitate.
I have already
made the first steps
toward work of this type.
I commanded
my living brushes
by remote control.

Epithalamium

For Benjamin La Rocco and Linnea Paskow on May 30th, 2011

Now oceanic span
    in ikon silo
        pose koan praise

Oilcan airman joins woman limner in romance aisle

(I will)

O Enamor Owl
O Manila Animal
O Enamel Llama
Our paws poke limber oracle

Lions unseal carmine wines
    Lemon sake
        Roman ales

Plink plonk polka bolero
Canal skoal opens melon arbor
Pink piano spins miracle romance
Nacre piano spins banjo clamor
Maroon ocarina boreal paean
Awaken lips on noble jerboa
Arcane merlin inner ninja
Join raccoon lapis on acorn isle
Pines croon in bloom combo

Inks link winks on camera
Amenable nameable linen amble
Enable balm élan jam
Walk swap plan lips speak

Anima Brain Cornea
Spoken plain
BE A POEM

O Pin Yin Sonnet (4)

Plus I don't understand their food.
Who eats chicken feet and eggs
buried in mud is unwholesome.
Something dirty slithers along
in their uncleanliness you see what
no one is saying is how many of them
like to eat animals that got no eyes
some kind of in-between thing.
Plus what kind of people eat six-
legged creatures and dried duck blood.
You know there is something not right about
putting frogs and grasshoppers together.
They aren't friends on earth—so why
serve them at the same dinner.

O Pin Yin Sonnet (11)

There is no room for them horizontally
vertically, or in a jar: glass or ceramic
Even these have started to take up too much room
The confiscation of coffins and urns is a top priority
We must stop the practice of filling the ground
where there should be factories and high-rises
From now on the dead must be cremated and their ashes
Scattered in a vegetable patch, or by the side of the road
where they once sat, watching trucks rumbling past
or scattered on lakes and ponds, wherever they leave
no sign of having once taken up space and now dissatisfied
wish to leave some part of their husk behind, stubborn coots
who think their time has not come to an ignoble end
We must pulverize and scatter them and the customs they cling to

O Pin Yin Sonnet (13)

"Don't blame bat soup for the Wuhan virus."

They don't just gobble down four-legged and two-legged creatures
They slurp slime-depositing life-forms residing on pond bottoms
They bury their eggs in dirt dug up from children's graveyards
They make broth for dumpling soup from bones of rabid dogs
They scrape donkey hides and turn the piles of pickings into youth jelly
They rub bird droppings into dark crevices in pursuit of yellow beauty
They refuse to change their names to soft letters that roll off the tongue
They hide others among them that harbor torrents of bad and ugly feelings
They claim their ancestors were inventors when they were farmers crouching in mud
They concoct histories so fantastical that not even small children believe them
They invented fireworks, noodles, and kung fu, which hardly adds up to a civilization
They openly sneeze and snicker about it and then scatter like mice
They are nothing more than scribbled names on the flyleaf of a tattered book
They might make good sneakers but they are sneakier than snakes

O Pin Yin Sonnet (16)

"My message is that let's get back to work.
Let's get back to living.
Let's be smart about it."

—Texas Lt. Gov. Dan Patrick

The trouble with the Chinese is that they like their old people
the older the better, as if each one of those wrinkled excuses
was a bottle of fine wine, which they know *nada* about
the Chinese got it all wrong: boatloads of their grandparents
should be more than happy to die from coronavirus
It's a cost-effective way to save their grandchildren from being poor
That's why there is something deeply wrong with China and the Chinese
They believe getting old and not working and sitting around toothless
is proof of love, but it is not; old Chinese are just grinning vampires
sucking the marrow from their young and packing them off to factories
Americans know better: that's why they go to the beach and play golf
Americans invented plastic surgery, tight pants, and rock 'n' roll
What have the Chinese done besides give us cookies crammed with lies?
We really know how to live, while the Chinese don't even know how to die

O Pin Yin Sonnet (18)

(Definitions for Joseph Donahue and Albert Mobilio)

A Senator is a larval form known to sprawl in leather chairs
A wet market is where you go to buy a bucket of unwashed food
A laboratory is what you need to coil together more diseases
A car is the rickshaw you drive when you cannot leave town
A hair salon is a mirror where you breed more germs
A restaurant is a table that lets you sneeze into the food
A President is an elected official who cannot tell the truth to his children
A Secretary of State is a poncho in charge of manufacturing rumors
A housing complex is where you go to die among friends
A sweatshop is one way to help shoppers save money
A whistleblower goes to jail for crimes others commit
A scientist is a shaved baboon who fits neatly into a lab coat
A buffoon is a person who believes the President first
A patriot is often identified by his or her misspelled tattoos

O Pin Yin Sonnet (21)

I watched the old man, who is not that old, fall harder than he was pushed
The police walked by because they had seen this act before, many times
They teach it in Chinese circus and acrobat school, an easy trick to get an AHH
I watched the old man, a well-known agitator, a member of a terrorist group
He was carrying something in his hand, a device, probably made in China
Maybe the device sent the wrong signal, causing him to fall backward
That is because Chinese don't read from left to right, but, get this, from right to left
I watched the old man fall, but was the blood coming from his head really his
All you need is a bag you can squeeze and everyone will think you are dying
I watched the old man, who is not that old, act like he had been pushed
after running into the police, tripping over his big feet, and falling backward
One moment he was standing, the next moment he was on the ground bleeding
You don't get that way by being pushed; you get that way by falling
I watched the old man, who is not so old, fall before he was almost pushed

O Pin Yin Sonnet (26)

We want to be rambunctious and harass anyone who is slow
One way is to play tag with old people and shout at them
They are easy to pick out and they aren't going anywhere
You just need one and the really round ones make good posts
They are fat and slow because they eat fatteners and don't exercise
Imagine one of them trying to run; it might almost make you cry
when standing outside and laughing with friends is more amusing
Only old people and those with weak immune systems die from it
What's wrong with a little horseplay—we're just having some fun
It's always in the back of my mind that the world is freaking out
It's not like they have anything better to do in the summer sun
You can't start sobbing because gray wrinkled people croak from it
It makes a great plot for a revenge film that all the young dream of
It's another good reason to gather outside, drink and sneer

O Pin Yin Sonnet (28)

They cannot say that they invented the atom bomb
They keep crickets in cages and listen to frogs
They don't like to use a knife and fork
They don't drink milk and prefer to eat pigs
They use a different horoscope than the one in the Sunday newspaper
They cry when no one is looking and they don't count their tears
They don't write words that can be translated into English
They brush in their suns with dusty black ink
They know how to stop juices from flowing to the brain
They claim to have invented spaghetti but they don't eat waffles
They like to keep their old people alive as long as possible
They venerate the dead as if they were still sitting beside you
They spit on the sidewalk while talking with their friends
Their hair is great for wigs and they are good at manicuring

Written in the Shadows Cast by *The Burning of the Houses of Lords and Commons* (1835) by J. M. W. Turner

1.

At one point in the story the rain was green, and the sky was pink shot through with painterly streaks of mauve and gray. Everyone, including the servants and maids, went onto the verandah and began applauding. It wasn't yet evening.

Even those who were on the outside of the narrative— those like us, who had no place in the story—were invited to attend this momentous event.

Along the riverbanks the fulsome reflections of flowers blossomed in every imaginable hue. Some colors floated slowly toward the sky, like boats ferrying the dead to their destination. Twisted mazes of sparks led the way.

It was a celebration, an announcement of dread and joy. We were lost within a swirling storm of seraphic color, dripping with the revelations the sky had flung in our faces. That's when it came to our attention that the palace was on fire, but no one dared cross the river and approach its gates.

This was a different story, its narrative promising that the construction and destruction of civil order would occur naturally, like the weather or the flags flying within it.

This was the story none of us were invited to attend, unless we already had taken up residence in its chapters, with its stained pages rising toward the fiery ceiling the architect had told them would be blue forever.

This was the story that did not invite intervention.

2.

Just as there are two paintings, with many witnesses huddled on the far shore, there are at least two stories and those who weren't invited to listen to them.

This story happened before we met. No one but us remembers it now, two shadows standing beneath a stone arch, a dark river flowing past.

What does it mean to be alone with each other, sharing memories no one else has?

Or perhaps this is the story that cannot be addressed, the one that started with and without our consent, the one we are still telling, the one in which we become honorary citizens of a city not yet named.

Inhabitants of a small city, a hovel in the sky.

As it is, we are spoonfuls of ashes scattered among the day's abominations.

We will never be sure how our voices intersected amidst the pillars constantly being erected for and against prismatic densities by which one is supposed to swear lifelong allegiance.

Such alliances seemed based on a different astrology than the one guiding us through the night. There is another set of stars in the sky and we don't know their names or their purpose. That is what is pulling us across the burning lake.

This was a dream which one of us later told the other. Or dreamed of telling the other, as the difference between these two types of flying having dissolved long ago.

Each of us lay there thinking: I wish I could say something about our future that will come true.

3.

A room each of us wanted to erect, a story or shelter, against the wind that untethered us from everything we tried to hold onto, from concrete nodes to abstract ideas.

Each of us needed that shaded plateau, that place where sensual asides could unfold without interruption.

On the small shelves on which we pretended to sleep, when vast constellations of villainous orthography prowled the land, looking for components to evaporate into bursts of fiery laughter, we realized the world was porous, and that we were handfuls of sand trickling through its openings into the sea waiting below.

How to hold onto ourselves and each other without threatening the seedlings beneath the skin?

In the beginning we told ourselves there was an exit, somewhere for us to begin making up what had never happened and, in all likelihood, never would.

Later, we told each other in one way or another that there was a window with a view of paradise. We silently agreed that the window doesn't open because it was never there, but that the shadows of its imprint could be seen on the opposite wall. Some days we sit facing them, trying to decipher their promises, but more often than not, we look the other way, still believing that there is something else we need to see.

Firefly Promises

1.

Each of us began in midsentence, wiring frayed, blue electricity filling the air. Motion whispers anyone could see through if they stopped to look. This is the snapshot I see when I close my eyes. Faded music. Rush of disclosures followed by missives delivered in an electronic suitcase.

Walking on either side of the river of self-loathing, learning not to step into it, though we slip, and it is unavoidable. Later learning the names of those missteps so as not to make them again, though often did, as each said to the other in the future imperfect, from across the stream that widens and thins according to a tarot deck whose cards are never seen.

Reasons or excuses—which will we run out of first? Did we know when we started that the river was between us and that we drank from it, seeing not our reflection, but that of someone we didn't wish to resemble, even if we did. Some of this is real and some of this is oxygen. Details are crumbs and scabs to be picked at. A subsistence diet one could grow fat on.

What do you do with the fumes, the fuming, while scampering up the ladders of assuming? What disdain greets you, happy to welcome you home? What question that is already answered shall be asked of you next? Where is the rest of the bruised honey? Whose relic have you become? Why try on what doesn't spare you?

What was I just saying or thinking to say to you, the words hesitant, a smokestack unfolding its letters to the sky, which is always hurrying to the bus station full of wickedness and fast food? Am I capable of saying this? Or even this? Other than in midsentence, how I shall continue—knowing there is no end in sight.

This is not what the river told me would happen.

2.

It is said that this is a human space we occupy, but today I am not so sure.

I wonder if we are in it or it is in us—a verb and a noun that have yet to announce their shapes or directions. Are we adrift or simply drifting?

Did we know that we would reveal ourselves so quickly? Did we know we would lead each other over valleys of pain because we didn't try to cover them, nor find any reason to call attention to their presence—they weren't monuments after all.

Sympathy wasn't what we wanted. That's what everyone asks for, a quick salve to bathe the deep ruins. It was as if all we wanted to do was start at the beginning and talk. Is such a beginning possible?

Had we guessed that other sentences would follow the first slow greeting, and the unexpected comfort of talking that began filling the air between you and I, between all the pronouns we occupied and abandoned?

Had we ever thought that it might be possible to talk about the pronouns we left behind, shed, buried, drove away, got rid of in a hurry? Or whisper about the ones we still carried with us?

Had we imagined the growing cascades filling missives sent from miles away, to someone sitting or driving, moving along a road the other would never see.

The only thing that holds us together are the missives we send each other.

Some days the words seem even more real than we are.

It was as if I had never talked to anyone before. Or, it was that I had never talked to you before—talked to someone who seemed so open to what I was saying that the words appeared to fly through you. Your answers were not words, at least as I thought I knew them. They plunged into me, and they stayed wherever I looked. I began hearing them playing back.

I imagine this is what it must have been like for Odysseus when he had his crew tie him to the mast—music that not even music could describe. He must have kept hearing their notes long after the island vanished beneath the horizon. Was that a crazy smile that kept blossoming on his face?

3.

You have become a figment of my imagination telling me that whatever I wish for must remain unspoken. It is true that humans do not live on love alone. Bread and whiskey do not cover the rent. What do we become but scowling vacuum cleaners trying to clean the mess we have made of our daily existence. The telltale crumbs of pointillist loathing are only part of the widening story that no one wants to tell.

The rest are gestures, celebrated poems, overactive prurience.

I decide it is better if I send a letter than a poem, a dream instead of a fiction, something dropped into the sea. This is by no means a testimony trudging ashore. Not even a poet's ego should be that grandiose.

Rather, it is a small corner of the page that I am trying to take up, a corner of a corner. On it I have written that one day I will watch you sleeping in my clothes. I don't know where this thought came from, but I have refused to put it away.

4.

I am copying down what I am being told to write. It is not a voice I hear, yours or mine or anyone else's, but the space between words that seems to fill with other words, other indications, hints or hums—a kind of music that words cannot accompany, falling away from their small handles on the world, like leaves on a windy day.

I am copying down what I am being told to write, but I keep thinking these are my words, not someone else's, that I am thinking and saying and sending to you. And yet it's not you that I am writing to, is it? It is my idea of you, my dream, illusion or glimpse. A string of silhouettes.

This can only mean that this is my ode to failing to write a poem worthy of your attention. Am I extolling you or extirpating words that are poor exposures of the quandary of pronouns you tell me constitute some of the parameters of your inexhaustible inferno?

Is this what it means to fall out of the unauthorized sky? Is this what it means to be a feather borne by the wind, or a cloud of thwarted eagerness? What brought us to this ocean of loneliness in which we can hear each other swimming in the distance?

From Black Threads from Meng Chiao 1.

2.

Shall I float this poem on the river
to meet you

past the radiant light of oil refineries
the red neon glow of words rising above the horizon

past furniture outlets and cargo ships
lovers drifting towards the gorge

Shall I point this poem past weeds and overpasses
tents and chairs

past courtyards and parking garages
named after mythical animals

Shall I place this poem
on the swirling black river

in the last daylight hours
watching it turn

into clouds, mist and rain

3.

My room is filling
with butterflies and snow

An armless clock
cannot move slower

I don't need to part
the curtains

to know the sky behind it
is also black-and-white

a photograph of
a photograph

you sent me
via telepathic means

Whenever I close
my eyes

I hear rain's exploding
stars and tears

A photograph of you
burns its candle in my brain

I sit alone in my room
waiting for a poem

to appear in the shadows
I crawl into my tiny bed

a poet sleeping next to a cloud
I fill page after page with words

In the morning the paper is blank

This is how I send you my poems

written in dirt with a stick

From Black Threads from Meng Chiao 2.

1.

In the bad translation of the Chinese poem
that I have all but forgotten

two lovers drift downstream in a boat
fashioned from ivory or teak

yellow tar or bald tires
an unlikely substance

which is true of love poems
written in a distant era

In purple mountains
populated by solitary archers

unemployed animal trainers
hermit poets searching for a lasting rhyme

I spend all day
talking to my shadow

It is winter or summer
I cannot remember which

Oil refineries send their candle flames jetting toward the moon
that old pearl

2.

I cannot
pen my shadow
to the page

Once the ink is dry
there will be no one
to read this poem

I might as well
count the leaves
falling from the sky

3.

Spring left when
I was not looking

Your beautiful translation
only makes my poem worse

Turning a few scattered lines
into fish darting beneath rocks

I heard you whispering to yourself
while the lovers drifted out of sight

Can you follow that red thread of sky
past junkyard piled with secondhand coffins

Petals from this poem
fall into black eddies

Weren't you once also a thick blue shadow
floating through the gorge

A column of snowy egrets
vanishes into the sun

If there was something
you could have held onto

what would it have been

Egyptian Sonnet (1)

Don't be vexed, dear jackals
Look upon this pavilion night,
where wounded statues murmur
unutterable things, and words
circle themselves like broken satellites
Strange devices harnessed with wings,
let your pages charm the charmed of our brief time,
hunkered down in their glow-worm hermitage,
sparkling with carrion: stars as thick as flies
—subterranean cataract portal precipice bastion—
fall through rifts of sky, and black foam
covers our dented prow's painted eyes
O my beloved, look through your tears and your cries,
heaven still sits inside a gem copied
in pomegranate and vermilion

Egyptian Sonnet (2)

A hippo sits patiently in a palm tree
while a hoopoe hops up a ladder
On desert's edge, far from flickering
oil lamps, a Sloughi plays tag with jackals
a leopard herds gazelles and geese
with a jeweled flute, and a young lady rat,
sitting on a pearl throne, waits
for monkeys to slide forth their gifts
A lion and a fox visit a sick ibis
A hyena stops a goose from running
into its mouth, and panthers stand petrified
in front of a white cat ambling toward the library
The first idol was a goddess
with a body of a hippopotamus

Egyptian Sonnet (5)

Horizon helmet horse hierophant
Sun presses clay snakes back
into rows of snarling eyes
Bristles brings back their prey
Red tent clouds lifting wings
Blue wizardry of lizards falling from
mouth of lion mounted in umber sky
By the time you reached me, I was fading
Into paint; dust lips were all that remained
Moon's prim carcass, black star's
framed mirror pulled by chariot
Dog circle imprint shadow
I cannot stop and look back
I should have carved my name
into your face

Egyptian Sonnet (18)

As if awakened by a signal we cannot hear,
quivering tufts, flashing metallic plumage,
ibises practice stretching their necks.
Brown geese become old-fashioned governesses
and storks gather, like unemployed advisers
while pelicans turn into roughly piled
walls of yellow-pink stones,
stout professors, now philosophical
now screaming in argument
collecting fish after fish, just as children
cram berries in their pockets
Silver arrows darting into undergrowth
Some run on foot the whole way
The sea compels them to rise into air

Movie Night

We were eating the latest wave of migrant sausages mixed with rare spices on the black verandah of the *Flying Saucer Bar and Grill* when I heard someone telling you that there was a rumor that I had sex with you once, but, at that point in your life, you weren't paying attention to small interruptions, and that, despite the peaks and valleys one naturally must traverse, nothing untoward happened, though an event unfolded (call it the collision of time and space dotted with foreign objects), what it was no one can now recall, even though someone said that he had heard that I had set out on a journey from the far end of town to tell you that what had happened that day was better than anything that could be said about it, but this is a different person that is speaking, the one who wasn't in the backseat intersecting with you, upright in the dark, but was sitting hunched over in the front cavity, driving through villages and towns scattered beneath the stars, haphazard collections of artificial light squatting in the dark, swarmed over by nothing they can remember, as the vehicle careened past libraries, firehouses, and general stores, repositories locked up for the night, two people curled around each other, pushing themselves into that place where shedding is inevitable, no one gripping the steering wheel, as the malfunctioning starship wobbles deeper into the dark, but of course this isn't what happened the night it happened there were two bodies and many shadows (some of them benign) embracing them in the parking lot beneath a yellow streetlamp near a train station occupied by two puppets on stilts, in the distance a blue castle commanding all who could see it to obey, kneel before its authority, yes there are instances, even now, when a tessellated edifice appears on the horizon or a child with one leg and an old sword hobbles out into the street, not to be run over by the tram, all while the two of them or is it us are engaged in a criminal act, at least as such acts are defined by the owner of the castle, a bald figurine whose corkscrew mouth never stops twisting, even in sleep, can't you hear what is happening outside, lightning on the rim of the world, arrival of thunder, the bowling alley shaking under the weeping willow, and there we are in the middle of a sentence that joins us and won't let go, and the longer we stay in this sentence, this rain, the more gets poured out of the containers that constitute our separate physical manifestations, including those things that we have never said to ourselves before, which is how all this got started.

Overnight

In Memory of Paul Violi (1944–2011)

I did not realize that you were fading from sight
I don't believe I could have helped with the transition

You most likely would have made a joke of it
Did you hear about the two donkeys stuck in an airshaft

I don't believe I could have helped with the transition
The doorway leading to the valleys of dust is always open

Did you hear about the two donkeys stuck in an airshaft
You might call this the first of many red herrings

The doorway leading to the valleys of dust is always open
The window overlooking the sea is part of the dream

You might call this the first of many red herrings
The shield you were given as a child did not protect you

The window overlooking the sea is part of the dream
One by one the words leave you, even this one

The shield you were given as a child did not protect you
The sword is made of air before you knew it

One by one the words leave you, even this one
I did not realize that you were fading from sight

The sword is made of air before you knew it
You most likely would have made a joke of it

After I Turned Sixty-Five

I start asking my coworkers if any of them want to rub my invisible tattoos
I tell neighbors to ponder clarity as if it is something that can be grasped
I pretend to be an insubordinate squirrel at family gatherings
I memorize how to be vile in different languages
I take up designer drugs and change my taste in music
I secretly keep track of all the people who call me "Pops"
I burn down my childhood tenement in a gentle fashion
I try different styles and flavors and announce that none of them suit me
I call a halt to all relationships that smack of the personal
I babble whenever someone asks me for directions
I tell lies about my adolescence in order to impress strangers with my pain
I learn to make the sounds of a man who is happily surprised
I insulate myself with voice mail and incompetence

Music from Childhood

You grow up hearing two languages. Neither fits your fits
Your mother informs you "moon" means "window to another world."

You begin to hear words mourn the sounds buried inside their mouths
A row of yellow windows and a painting of them

Your mother informs you "moon" means "window to another world."
You decide it is better to step back and sit in the shadows

A row of yellow windows and a painting of them
Someone said you can see a blue pagoda or a red rocket ship

You decide it is better to step back and sit in the shadows
Is it because you saw a black asteroid fly past your window

Someone said you can see a blue pagoda or a red rocket ship
I tried to follow in your footsteps, but they turned to water

Is it because I saw a black asteroid fly past my window
The air hums—a circus performer riding a bicycle towards the ceiling

I tried to follow in your footsteps, but they turned to water
The town has started sinking back into its commercial

The air hums—a circus performer riding a bicycle towards the ceiling
You grow up hearing two languages. Neither fits your fits

The town has started sinking back into its commercial
You begin to hear words mourn the sounds buried inside their mouths

Midway

I did not write a hauntingly beautiful book
No one was haunted by the words I wrote
Neither they nor the book were beautiful

I did not write a book in which the personal
And political converge. I did not become more
Somber and mature as the years sped by

I did not write poems that were desperate
Bewildered or astonished. I did not plumb the depths
In search of a moral encounter with human principles

I did nothing to revive poetic architectures
I did not take pains to ensure my poems performed
Against a backdrop of political, social and ethical values

I did not write a book in which themes and images
Resurface, satisfying the reader who, by now, has become
Increasingly anxious and is in need of comfort

I did not write my poems in either a plain or high style
I did not try to motivate the reader to tears or action
My writing is not considered remarkable for its spiritual force

My poems do not travel across a landscape of cultural memory
They do not strike a dynamic balance of honesty,
Emotion, intellectual depth, and otherworldly resonance

They will not startle you out of your daily anesthesia
They do not map the deepest crevices of the interior self
They cast no light on history's margins, overlooked and neglected

Nor is it sacrilegious to comment on my poems
What they lack, their absence of resonant wit,
What they fail to fulfill, worlds they miss out on

Section 6
(2021–2023)

Hearsay Song

They are dying out and I want to reach them before they are gone
Not that I know what I would say to them when I get there
Their songs rippling beneath temporary sky
As I approach, as I am doing now
Even though I am nowhere near wherever they are
Swirling in blossoming dust and dreaming they are not

They are dying out and I want to reach them before they are gone
Just as I want to reach myself before I too am gone
Another blossom sliding into slime
What notes do I hear drenched in fiery sky
Are these ghosts rising up before me
Or gasps of dust near a lake covered by algae

They are dying out and I want to reach them before their names vanish
Before they become ghosts dying in pink algae and ruined vowels
Not that I know what their songs say
Telling sting of monstrous human torrent
Wheeling above burning story of lost lives
Tapering branches of smoke, red and yellow leaves falling

They are dying out and I want to reach them
Before my name joins theirs in plastic matrimony
Before a blue-eyed undertaker powders my nose
Or I turn to powder in squirt gun of unprofitable insects
Secrets folded away never rinsed in scum corner
History erasing traces of its nothing new

On Being Told that I Don't Look and Act Chinese

I am deeply grateful for your good opinion
I am honestly indignant
I am, I confess, a little discouraged
I am inclined to agree with you
I am incredulous
I am in a chastened mood
I am far more grieved than I can tell you
I am naturally overjoyed
I am not going to let you pay me idle compliments
I am not in the least surprised
I am not sure I can manage it
I am persuaded by your candor
I am quite discomfited
I am so glad you think that
I am sorry to disillusion you
I can assure you it is most painful to me to hear you say it like that
I can easily understand your astonishment
I can only tell you the bare facts
I detest exaggeration
I don't know quite why you would say that
I hadn't thought of it in that light
I have never heard it put so well
I see it from a different angle
I stand corrected

After I Turn Sixty-Eight

I find distasteful ways to use the words "enduring" and "hopeful"
I begin stockpiling my daily doses of radiation in an abandoned dollhouse
I order crystals from mail order spiritual specialists and bury them in the front yard
I start telling my neighbors that I am interested in marrying an older mermaid
I ask a coworker if it is unsanitary to sneeze into my unwashed armpits
I confess to the druggist that the condoms are for my besotted dog
I tell the taxi driver that I was lucky to have escaped from the morgue
I shrug my shoulders and pretend that I don't know what you are saying
I ask people if they have seen any strange pedestrians wandering around, dazed
I carry a toy phone under my arm and talk into it whenever I go outside
I once told my psychiatrist that I speak gibberish in four different languages
I pretend that I am poet interested in discarded library books and obscure rhymes
I always sign the guest book with three X's because growing old is pornographic

After I Turn Sixty-Nine

I don't imagine that a chariot is hurrying near but that a sleek car is speeding up
I have started a list of the costumes I want to be buried in, beginning with horny centaur
I try to put aside obituaries but I am unable to do so for very long (maybe ten minutes)
I eat the same meal night after night while reading recipes of dishes I have never tasted
I shudder nearly every time I read the phrase "Lifetime Guarantee or Your Money Back"
I no longer find it necessary to stop and look at what is going on at a construction site
I decide I won't tell people to stop sending me books even if I will never read them
I stop and watch ambulances trying to get past cars that don't want to move aside
I begin thinking about different methods I might use to remove myself from the story
I know what my friend meant when he said his dog would take his place on the couch
I think about the cities I will never return to, including Cadaqués and Caracas
I wonder when I will no longer begin a poem with the words "if" and "when"
I dream that my ashes will be scattered in a remote spot in Ireland that no one visits
I admit that shrinking into myself is not as unpleasant as I once thought

Confessions of a Recycled Shopping Bag

I used to be a plastic bottle

I used to be scads of masticated wattle

I used to be epic spittle, AKA septic piddle

I used to be a pleasant colleague

I used to be a radiant ingredient

I used to be a purple polyethylene pony

I used to be a phony upload project

I used to be a stony blue inhalant

I used to be a family size turquoise bucket

I used to be a domesticated pink bubble

I used to be a pleasant red collagen

I used to be a beaming cobalt emollient

I used to be a convenient chartreuse antidepressant

Variation on a Line by Duo Duo

I love the house on fire
inviting us to lie down

Inviting us to become
its tightly fitting roof

As if the moon is a python
waiting to uncoil

As if our blushing cheeks
did not offer brazen proof

I love the house on fire
inviting us to lie down

Umber summer falling
slowly to its knees

Inviting us to lie down
in its scarlet tracks

Inviting us to embrace
the already blazing sky

In Memory of My Parents

Streets of Shanghai (1927)
Back from Shanghai (1929)
The Ship from Shanghai (1930)
Shanghai Express (1932)
Charlie Chan in Shanghai (1935)
West of Shanghai (1937)
Exiled to Shanghai (1937)
Shadows over Shanghai (1938)
North of Shanghai (1939)
Halfway to Shanghai (1942)
The Shanghai Cobra (1945)
The Lady from Shanghai (1947)
The Last Ships from Shanghai (1949)

The Congressman's Explanation

If you live in your car, I don't have to worry about you not being able to pay rent
If you eat scraps from a dumpster, I don't have to worry about you stealing food
You don't deserve to put in your miserable mouth and fumbling with your rotting teeth
If you find temporary employment in a warehouse so big
That no one remembers your name
I don't have to worry about you thinking your life is shit
Others with name tags will help you reach that conclusion
And if they have any brains sitting fat inside their misshapen skulls
They will inform you that you should have been left out in the rain
Because you didn't save for a rainy day
It's the American way—everyone gets what they merit
You got here on your own, didn't you?
Is it my fault that you failed miserably at being human?
That you became another blossoming eyesore on the scrubbed face of this great nation
There is a good reason that you were drubbed and you know
Deep in your worm-riddled heart that you got what you earned
If you live in your car, I don't have to worry about where you will sleep at night
If you live in your car, I won't have to concern myself
With where you will be found once you are dead
Another petty thought that takes up too much of my precious day
When I have the untrammeled happiness of my constituents to think about
If you live in your car, I don't have to worry about the next election
Because you will be gone, one way or another

The President's Second Telegram

Unfortunately, early reports of school not looking good
Unfortunately, this loss of decades has been going on too long
We're with you forever in the sadness school
We're affected by this absolutely terrible heartbreak hour
We send our love to everyone affected by our country
We send the loss of life our horrific deadly forever
We grieve for years of heartbreak in this tragic attack

(May 18, 2018)

A Painter's Thoughts (1)

After William Bailey (1930–2020)

I want to paint in a way that the "I" disappears into the sky and trees
The idea of a slowed down, slowly unfolding image held my attention

Variations on a theme are of no interest. A bowl and cup are not ideas.
I want my painting to be what it contains: it should speak, not me

The idea of a slowed down, slowly unfolding image held my attention
I paint things made of clay, just as the pigments I use come from the earth

I want my painting to be what it contains: it should speak, not me
Brown and ochre stoneware bowls beside a white porcelain pitcher

I paint things made of clay, just as the pigments I use come from the earth
I place the pale eggs on a dark, unadorned tabletop and let them roll into place

Brown and ochre stoneware bowls beside a white porcelain pitcher
The dusky red wall is not meant to symbolize anything but itself

I place the pale eggs on a dark unadorned tabletop and let them roll into place
I want to paint in a way that the "I" disappears into the sky and trees

The dusky red wall is not meant to symbolize anything but itself
Variations on a theme are of no interest. A bowl and cup are not ideas.

A Painter's Thoughts (3)

After Suzan Frecon

All decisions are made for visual reasons. The cathedral is finally anonymous
Made of multiple dimensions that go on and on. Even the sky temporarily recedes

I wish to strengthen the painting, make it exist, so that we will want to keep looking
When I traveled, I observed the vast range of red earths in the land and architecture

Made of multiple dimensions that go on and on, even the sky temporarily recedes
Red earth has been used throughout time: there are dots and handprints in caves

When I traveled, I observed the vast range of red earths in the land and architecture
My daughter, the poet, was reading excerpts from a Chinese poem over the phone

Red earth has been used throughout time: there are dots and handprints in caves
I think they are most successful when you can't say they look like something

My daughter, the poet, was reading excerpts from a Chinese poem over the phone
I would love it if I could capture something comparable in my paintings

I think they are most successful when you can't say they look like something
I grew up on an orchard, I was eating plums, and the colors stayed in my mind

I would love it if I could capture something comparable in my paintings
All decisions are made for visual reasons. The cathedral is finally anonymous

I grew up on an orchard, I was eating plums, and the colors stayed in my mind
I wish to strengthen the painting, make it exist, so that we will want to keep looking

A Painter's Thoughts (4)

After Catherine Murphy

My work is about looking very intently—the little curve that follows me
The difference now is that I might dream of an image that I want to do

I woke up as I was putting the blanket on the ground. I understood why I loved it
I am an observer, not a storyteller. I make narratives based on metaphor

When I see something that I want to do, nothing stops me from doing it
Some people want to make the equation narrower, but I want to make it larger

I am an observer, not a storyteller. I make narratives based on metaphor
I want the viewer to understand that this is a painting, not life

Some people want to make the equation narrower, but I want to make it larger
It was written down in a ledger that I was going to be put here to make those paintings

I want the viewer to understand that this is a painting, not life
The form repeats itself, but if I repeat a subject, I would have betrayed it

It was written down in a ledger that I was going to be put here to make those paintings
I could make very pretty brushstrokes, but they have no electrical meaning for me

The form repeats itself, but if I repeat a subject, I would have betrayed it
My work is about looking very intently—the little curve that follows me

I could make very pretty brushstrokes, but they have no electrical meaning for me
I woke up as I was putting the blanket on the ground. I understood why I loved it

A Painter's Thoughts (6)

(after Peter Saul)

I was searching my brain for some unexpected subject matter
I'm 86 and in grave danger of appearing elderly and demented

Unless you can come up with some subject you haven't done, even as a child
Flowers, for example, I haven't looked at them, much less painted them

I am 86 and in grave danger of appearing elderly and demented.
I am avoiding the reality that in a mere 14 years I'll be dead

Flowers, for example, I haven't looked at them, much less painted them
I got right to work, the usual careless distortions, on purpose or not

I am avoiding the reality that in a mere 14 years I'll be dead
It turns out that flowers are just as good subjects as flying saucers

I got right to work, the usual careless distortions, on purpose or not
It doesn't matter that nobody's fooled, because I am at least artistically

It turns out that flowers are just as good subjects as flying saucers
Right now, I'm thinking of God and Superman battling it out above an American city

It doesn't matter that nobody's fooled, because I am at least artistically
Who wants to think about how much will be destroyed at a time like this

Right now, I'm thinking of God and Superman battling it out above an American city
I was searching my brain for some unexpected subject matter

Who wants to think about how much will be destroyed at a time like this
Unless you can come up with some subject you haven't done, even as a child

A Painter's Thoughts (7)

(after Lois Dodd)

It is someone else's subject if you think it would look good if they painted it
If I work on this painting longer, it would be perfect and no longer mine

I am with my thin paint. Putting on a second coat will shut out the light
Morandi's paintings are wonderful, but they have not influenced me

If I work on this painting longer, it would be perfect and no longer mine
I admire juicy paint on other people's canvases, but that's not what I do

Morandi's paintings are wonderful, but they have not influenced me
Even if I never tell a story, my feelings and emotions will come through

I admire juicy paint on other people's canvases, but that's not what I do
In the beginning it was cows, just cows. Now it's human beings

Even if I don't tell a story, my feelings and emotions will come through
I don't want fancy stuff, or even a lot of stuff. Don't blame the abstract artists for this

In the beginning it was cows, just cows. Now it's human beings
I don't like distant views; I wouldn't be happy going to the top of a mountain

I don't want fancy stuff, or even a lot of stuff. Don't blame the abstract artists for this
The easel was there, I thought, well, this is fun: here I am painting myself painting.

I don't like distant views; I wouldn't be happy going to the top of a mountain
It is someone else's subject if you think it would look good if they painted it

The easel was there, I thought, well, this is fun: here I am painting myself painting
I am with my thin paint. Putting on a second coat will shut out the light

Hotel Jane Alice Peters

I like sitting in hotel lobbies that are as big as the apse of a cathedral and strung with Christmas lights. I like it when my posterior sinks into the cushion provided by the hotel management for exactly this encounter between lower extremity and nuanced comfort. I like letting my spine and all the flesh that surrounds it fall back into the carefully rounded, slightly tilting support that is attached to an elevated pairing of horizontal cushions that rests securely on four elegantly turned legs. I like the silver claws that form the chair's feet. I like knowing the architecture of this assembly was constructed with human ease in mind. I like pretending that I belong in a lobby festooned with polished brass fixings reminiscent of another era, or framed by fluted marble columns harkening back to an even earlier era. I like knowing I can travel back in time.

This is when I start replaying my favorite interlude, when I begin dreaming of meeting Carole Lombard, who died in a plane crash in Mount Potosi, Nevada, aged 33. This happened on January 16, 1942. Today is January 17, 2019, more than seventy-five years later. Is there a hotel in Mount Potosi? Is it named after Lombard, third wife of Clark Gable?

I like burrowing inside the extinct topography resurrected by young hotel designers, their manufactured version of our collective longing. I like their efforts to harness the barely controllable desire we have to step away from the time we inhabit into a hologram sector that has not been overrun by apocalyptic data. I like knowing that the scar a car accident left on Lombard's face could not be completely erased, and that we can see its trace on her cheek—like a horizon line—when the camera moves in close, as in *Hands Across the Table* (1935), costarring the charmless Fred MacMurray. I like knowing that she did not want to simper prettily or scream in terror on the screen. I like knowing that the "e" was added onto her name by mistake and that she decided to keep it. I like knowing that she took life as it came, even if I am not of that ilk and do not want to go down that tortuous path.

A View of the Tropics Covered in Ash

I began lying to myself at regular intervals, stopping by the side of the road only when it was necessary. The vegetation did not improve even as the interludes of pleasant shrubbery and herbaceous plants changed, and the waterfalls eventually became walls smothered in stains. I got tired of following myself back to the place where I was delivered; a howling newborn already indoctrinated that the mandibles of doom awaited me, along with other taunts and temptations too monstrous to mention. I did not have to sit long. We must all make dung, announced the boy with a smile full of crooked teeth. This was in the lobby where the first assignments were handed out. Where did you get those pearly gravestones screamed his toothless sister? What do you mean what do you mean moaned another vehicle headed for bedlam in an elastic waistband.

Life in an upscale suburb isn't bad once you get used to hell. The suburban pageantry of soccer played with plastic skulls and rapacious bugs on a green summer day is worthy of an opera, complete with pouting male and curvaceous diva. Drugstores that deliver licensed drugs and pastel condiments are not to be sneezed at. There are plenty of tonics guaranteed to cure baldness, but impotency is something to be proud of, since it means your contributions to civilization's convulsions are dwindling at an accelerated rate.

This is the time to begin concentrating on flying carpets, inexpensive episodes, and sitting in a rowboat on a speckled lake, dreaming of that moment long ago, when the first lie came to you unbidden. You are sleeping under a tree that reaches up past the bottom layer of starlit clouds. The lower branches are burning, just as you planned.

Unbidden

I never have been a pallbearer. I did not help carry the coffins of my mother or my father—they died a few months apart—to their adjacent unmarked plots in a fenced-in cemetery on a suburban street near Burlington, Massachusetts, where they and my brother moved after I graduated from high school. Twice, I selected a coffin and paid for it with my credit card, but I never felt the actual physical weight of their death.

It was a bright and sunny morning when my father called. An hour later I was carrying a large cardboard box to the post office. That is when I saw her and did not know what to say when—for the first time—she stopped in front of me, smiled and said: how are you?

We were standing close together, in a zone not quite penetrated by what was around us. We had been smiling at each for weeks, maybe longer—whenever we passed each other, usually on a Saturday on West Broadway when everyone was going to art galleries—but we had never stopped to say hello to each other before because one of us was always with someone else. I stood there and said: I am well. I am going to the post office and looked at the unwieldy box I was carrying. I gave her a weak smile and a shrug and I walked away and never saw her again.

I left that afternoon on a plane and made my way to my parents' house, a place I stayed in but where I never lived because I did not have a room there. I did not talk to anyone about what had happened. When she said hello and smiled, I was still hearing my father tell me that my mother had just died. He said that the last thing she said to him was how disappointed she was in me, and that I was clearly a failure for a son. A few moments later she had a heart attack and fell down the stairs. He had waited a long time to say these things to me in a calm, matter-of-fact voice, things my mother never said. I could hear him smiling loudly behind his report.

I stood there looking at a woman that I was smitten over and daydreamed about and all I could manage to do was mutter a few meaningless pleasantries.

I walked away.

I walked away wondering: is this what it means to be a poet?

You carry boxes to the post office.

You are tongue-tied and lost.

Whatever you want to say will not be said in this lifetime.

Too Far to Write Down

1.

I, humble scribe of clouds, ask permission to make my case
While you scatter ocher cumuli above circles of open huts
Pull thick violet brushstrokes through cascading green mountains
I watch my poems ferry fiery farewells downstream
Dream that I am in two places at once, listening
To new ghosts complain there is no room
Until the old ghosts leave their vestments behind
Hear wisps of weeping—wind gathering in mulberry trees
Become wrinkled sheet floating above empty bed
Watch victory and defeat unfurl flags against coal red sky
As moon follows its hollow twin into a waterfall's marbled sections
I turn into drops of ink and snow settling into the repaired space of this poem

2.

I, humble scribe of clouds, ask permission to make my case
It does not matter if the poem's eyes are those of a dead fish

It sees that I am an idle dreamer jilted by flowers stretching far
Sees me patch another layer of gauze to a mulberry tree eaten by moths
Sees me kneel by a river and look at a face waging war with itself, and long ago
I have become a dirty chair on which no one will sit, not even my stuffed parrot
Must I confess that I see you dancing in a poem that I have not yet written
This morning, I began washing away remnants of my cold mountain house
Can this memory become a blue flower floating in a pool of black ink
It is snowing in these poems, which were once branches catching the snow
Unreadable midnight, this part of the world you have not yet bid good-bye
I watch the river changing colors as if it can find inside itself another story to spill

3.

I, humble scribe of clouds, ask permission to make my case
Bamboo forest background, floating arrival, unfurling curlicues
Our ancestors named star clusters after remnants of earlier civilizations
Getting old is no longer a joke even if you have started to become one
I spend all night painting a single blue tear, which I scratch away in the morning
Winter's pewter sky is about to greet us with its roll call of gray
What if a sword can be brighter than the stars—neither will save me
After every rain, snails fill the center of my cottage
Infatuated by your candor, I crawl around my room looking for your shadow

It is like tying a poem to a pigeon's leg and watching it fly in circles
Falling deeper into my foolishness, I begin greeting the brushes and pens
I wake up with an erection and can no longer remember if there was another time

4.

I, humble scribe of clouds, ask permission to make my case
In anticipation of the future, I promise to forget everyone's name
The stars never offer enough clues, which we pick over, furiously, like birds
We want signs of reassurance with tidbits of pleasure strewn throughout
A carcass simmering at the bottom of a pot brought out at the end of every poem
Meanwhile, who will scout the path the painter has left for us to follow
Is the task of the poet to find new ways to turn despair into rice soup
Night settles on the other side of these gnarled mountains
The celestial courtyard where our ancestors sit, awaiting our arrival
Why didn't you write to me when I started bleeding through my paper heart
Who drew this motionless green river outside my window
What absurd errand have you sent me on, now that I have fallen back to earth

8.

I, humble scribe of clouds, ask permission to make my case
I have stopped listening to my thoughts, which are small and unfriendly

I followed you until I realized it was not you I was following

I don't love the blossoms enough that I want to catch them when they fall

In the distance a house sits beneath an approaching meteor of paint

I have not bathed in months and still I don't smell like I am alive

I don't need to try and remember the taste of dirt

A ragged string of birds is erasing itself in the folded mist

I am tempted to make sense, however brief and foolish that might seem

I climb a mountain bending beside a river and never leave my table

I set this poem beneath ink-patterned sky made of paper and stone

Whatever I have written on will be torn apart and covered over

Charles Baudelaire and I Meet in the Oval Garden

Which windowpane are you beating your wings against today?
I am not as stubborn as you: I am flying straight into that delicious fire.

Buckets of bubbling tar and champagne await us at the *Blue Chalet.*
Do you skip like this because you have been invited into our lovely little choir?

I am not as stubborn as you: I am flying straight into that delicious fire.
I thought you were going to the theater in your new cabriolet.

Do you skip like this because you have been invited into our lovely little choir?
Yes, I do know the difference between a martini and a matinee.

I thought you were going to the theater in your new cabriolet.
They say that the latest strain hiding in the shadows is a yellow vampire.

Yes, I do know the difference between a martini and a matinee.
You have your subdivisions and high rises, while I have my shire.

They say that the latest strain hiding in the shadows is a yellow vampire.
Don't worry—my ancestors are sewn up in overcoats and on full display.

You have your subdivisions and high rises, while I have my shire.
When it comes to curry and gin, I say: "Let's wallow in Combray."

Don't worry—my ancestors are sewn up in overcoats and on full display.
Which windowpane are you beating your wings against today?

When it comes to curry and gin, I say: "Let's wallow in Combray"
Buckets of bubbling tar and champagne await us at the *Blue Chalet.*

After I Turned Seventy-One

for Laura Mullen

I did not expect to see myself standing before a mirror

I look like someone I would never want to meet

I wonder if I have made a mistake without knowing it

I am sure the word "disaster" does not tell the whole story

I know there is room for improvement but I decide to skip over that part

I realize this passport is the last one that will be issued to me

I begin to think the joke is not only on me

I can walk in any direction and still end up in the wrong place

I stop trying to make a list of words I will never use again

I decide making sense is no longer an acceptable form of lying

I think it is prudent to let others do the counting

I often tell strangers that I might start vomiting when the seasons begin to change

I agree that "reincarnation" is a scam perpetuated by life insurance companies

I liked it when the cab driver called me "young man" and gave him a smaller tip

Chinatown Blues

Don't keep saying poetry makes nothing happen
I am not trying to be your surrogate chaplain

I am going to grow up and be a hatchet man
Doing the sharp and shiny thing—being the best I can

Don't tell me the wood is far too green or yellow
Or that Mr. Frost—protector of fences—is a jolly good fellow

I am still going to grow up and tell it slant
Don't even try and tell me I can't

Stop reminding me I have to watch what I say
Be polite or I will have to pay and pay

I am still going to grow and be a hatchet man
Doing the sharp and shiny thing—being the very best I can

From Li Shangyin Enters Manhattan

1.

I am a parakeet in a cave, malaise's candle flame,
An open letter to myself who is you: poets always
Need to be foreign, even in their own country
I was walking into a candy store when I bumped into
Another dance of ink I will never join in fragrant ceremony
Drips of soot filling clouds of yesterday's imagination
Can you sing "of" in a downloaded song and not sound
Like you are a native speaker lost in an alley
With two entrances, one of which is your mouth
I comb streets of sand and pollen, looking for flowers
Whose petals possess a remedy for dreams
Filled with poorly transcribed instructions guaranteed
To make every devourer wish life could be written in reverse
Do you know whose glossolalia you will be speaking in today

2.

The greatest poet in Chinese history
Is a mulberry tree on which poems
Are sprinkled in ash, ink, or snow
Walking to corner movie palace
Talking to ladybugs, humming rhymes
To radio operators, whistling standards
For plankton mechanics under pine sap sky
I stop and watch a clowder of polluted cats

Swimming upstream, in search of better furniture
I squat in a cold bath and imagine I am a poet
A talking tree writing sonnets for humankind
An atomic clock sitting on a rock in paradise
Announcing, this is the blue mirror in which
You will see yourself spinning all your fault lines

3.

Why do you say this scroll of painted mulberry bark
Is a trembling lake deaf to ink splashes and falling sun
Have you ever talked to coroners of silkworms
Children who only watch movies in rearview mirrors
Gardeners who tend to weeds growing through gravestones,
Waiters who refuse to serve real or substitute meat
What side of your face aches from obedience issues
What milestone did you reach when your heart
Turned to ash, and you wrote: "even the fog is blight"
Are poets still underpaid to operate levers of
A dead language machine, kill doves when
They think the festooned little plumps are laughing
More silver lacerations refilling night's placard bowl
Memory's janitors sweeping away sights of wounds and ruins

5.

More huts of blather retreat into latest urban sob story
Night arrives full of carbon stains in leaking tank
What winged shadow brushed against your diesel chariot
What upright little god of the hearth did you swear at today

Who requested extra sets of hands to squeeze birds
Squawking right out of life, their carbonated spit splintering the air,
Midnight hearse hauling their little crystal coffins back to
Seaweed banks, where you and your throttle of soulful bleeders
Have to sing for your package, no magnetic stripes please
That is the repeat glutton pressing the unheated lips of
Your baffled pocket mouth, your cold distress
Burn down legions of last overcoats, their headless shoes
There is nothing thicker than sickness dripping against
The blackened bulkhead of this gutted rickshaw

6.

I keep my remaining glands in a jar by the nightstand
I live in a condo villa and drink tall glasses of cold plum juice
Give me edible sermons and I will recycle your sentiments
Display another filament binge as I grind the heart loose
Pick slips of masticated plastic from plates of steaming viscera
These are slippery hills we are hooked forward to
Lumps and bones spilling lard of our common stock market
Lined with barnacles and crackling bunkum, courtesy of old world ways,
My name is Captain Manatee, Oboe Steam House, Elgin Relic,
I sing and fly in the opera known as the Lost United Fates
Picketed gates or heads on plates, weigh down upon
Stack of whitened swans, headline pileup with more bash-ins
Suspects speak of terminal clutter, but comic relief is when
You don't pee in your pants by a flooded highway

Elsa and Charles with Cameo by Tallulah

My favorite moment in *The Bride of Frankenstein* (1935), directed by James Whale, and starring Boris Karloff (naturally) as the Monster and frizzy-haired Elsa Lanchester (who also plays the author Mary Shelley at the start of the film) as his betrothed, is when the young bride looks up at her towering, misunderstood hubby and vehemently whispers: "I hate you, you oversized piece of imitation luggage." The monster begins crying at the sight of the young woman gyrating wildly before him, pounding his massive chest with her tiny fists, before reaching over and pulling a shiny black switch, which sends waves of sparking voltage shooting throughout the laboratory and Gothic tower where they are standing, turning it into a camera close-up of granite blocks, burning desks and papers, broken beakers, bottles of potions and powders, and what might be the mingling of the monster and his angry bride's limbs.

It does not matter that this did not happen in the film because it is very easy to imagine Lanchester doing something outrageous and memorable, as it was an epidemic running through her family. She was the daughter of James Sullivan and Edith Lanchester, socialists who refused to legalize their union in stuffy, rule-bound England, although they happily stayed together until one preceded the other in death without thinking that heaven awaited them. When Edith's family learned of her plans to live with James without being married in a church or standing before a magistrate (she was by then a confirmed atheist who believed "marriage" would deprive her of her freedom), they kidnapped her and had her certified as insane at the Priory Hospital in Roehampton. The cause of her "insanity" was listed as "overeducation." This did not deter Edith in the least, and the case caused a national scandal. According to the *New York Times,* Edith's incarceration "rivet[ed] the attention of three kingdoms" that "no penny paper had printed less than ten columns on this engrossing subject during the week" Edith was incarcerated and abused. After Edith was released, she got a job as the private secretary of Eleanor Marx, Karl Marx's daughter, who was well aware of the case and sought her out.

Before turning thirteen, Elsa had studied dance with Isadora and Raymond Duncan, taught dance to younger children in her neighborhood, and published a magazine to which she was the sole contributor. Later, she posed for the sculptor Jacob Epstein, who was born to Polish refugees on New York's Lower East Side. After he received money for his first commission, he moved to Paris, where he received his second commission, which was to design Oscar Wilde's tomb for the Père Lachaise Cemetery. When the tombstone was unveiled, the French declared it obscene and covered it with a cloth, doubly interring Mr. Wilde. Today, a glass barrier surrounds the tomb because so many people have drawn hearts and messages on it.

After posing for Epstein, Lanchester founded an after-theater nightclub, the Cave of Harmony, frequented by John Maynard Keynes, Evelyn Waugh, Tallulah Bankhead, and Aleister Crowley, who probably never sat at the same table, but should have. According to Lanchester, in her autobiography, *Elsa Lanchester Herself* (1983), Crowley rode a bicycle to the club and "his head was shaved and he wore a yellow kilt." She did not describe what Bankhead wore.

In *Lifeboat* (1944), directed by Alfred Hitchcock, Bankhead, who described herself as "pure as the driven slush," had to climb a ladder every morning to reach the water tank where the movie was being filmed, and where the rest of the cast was waiting for her to show up. When Bankhead arrived on the set a large crowd always quickly gathered around the water tank to watch her slowly ascend the ladder. To make her arrival and ascent memorable but without unnecessary fanfare, Bankhead thought it would be best to be discreet and simply wear no underwear. When a disconcerted witness brought Bankhead's personal peep show to Hitchcock's attention, he replied: "I don't know if this is a matter for the costume department, makeup, or hair dressing." But this all took place in Lanchester and Bankhead's future, which we have not yet reached.

In 1936, a year after being blown to smithereens by her ungainly monster husband, Lanchester returned to life to play Peter Pan in J. M. Barrie's play, *Peter Pan; or, The Boy Who Wouldn't Grow Up*, which was being performed to great applause at the London Palladium. Lanchester's real husband, Charles Laughton, played Captain Hook, who Barrie described as being "never more sinister than when he was being polite, which is probably the truest test of breeding." Lanchester and Laughton would go on to star together in twelve films, as well as act in Bertolt Brecht's play, *Galileo*, which was staged in Los Angeles in 1947, directed by Joseph Losey, who was born in La Crosse, Wisconsin, where he and Nicholas Ray were classmates at La Crosse Central High School.

While Lanchester and Laughton were parrying in *Peter Pan*, across the English Channel and beyond France, Belgium, and Netherlands, which hugged the coast, the Olympics were being held in Berlin, Germany, as they are now being held in Beijing, China, where you cannot buy Peking duck or publish poems critical of the government.

Years later, the black athlete Jesse Owens, who won four gold medals in Berlin, told a news reporter the greatest ovations he received in his lifetime were in that city, three years after Hitler and the Nazi Party had come to power, and not in America during the presidency of Franklin Delano Roosevelt. Although it is a myth that has been repeated many times because it is easier to believe than the truth, neither Hitler nor the Germans snubbed Owens. It was Roosevelt and America. When Owens returned to America he received no congratulations from President Roosevelt. There were seventeen Black American athletes at the 1936 Olympics. They won fourteen of the fifty-six medals awarded to the American athletes. None of them were invited to the White House.

I was reminded of *The Bride of Frankenstein*, the 1936 Olympics, Hollywood characters, poetry, and marriage, when I read this observation in John Houseman's review of her autobiography: "Miss Lanchester's memoirs are filled with [. . .] frank, vivid and sometimes tasteless impressions of friends and enemies [. . .].” Houseman’s remark followed Lanchester’s description of Brecht, who smoked cheap cigars and lived with her and Laughton during the rehearsal of *Galileo*: “passing through Brecht, the smoke came out with the sourest, bitterest smell. [. . .] He hadn’t many teeth and his mouth opened in a complete circle so you’d see two little tombstones sticking out of this black hole. A very unpleasant sight.”

Thinking of Lanchester’s description, I wondered if she and Laughton are interred in or around Los Angeles, in a cemetery that has the word “green” in it, lying side by side in perpetuity, something they seldom did in life.

Constance Dowling's Eyes

The seed of this story was planted in Turin in the early 1990s, after I met the reclusive artist Nicola De Maria, who, in the late 1980s, sent me one of his catalogs, *Parole Cinesi* (1985–86) (trans: Chinese Words) and a letter introducing himself. In the winter of 1988, after further correspondence, I flew to Milan and took a train to Turin, where I met Nicola at the station. That first afternoon we walked along the Po River and he recited the opening lines of "Howl" in English. The zoo was closed because of the cold. That was the beginning of our friendship, and over the next fifteen years we saw each other around a half dozen times, always in Turin.

I think the writer and gallerist Jean Frémon—who I met earlier—must have given Nicola my address. Frémon is a writer and was—in the 1980s—one of the three partners running Galerie Lelong & Co., which represented De Maria. The other partners were the poet and friend of Giacometti and Miró, Jacques Dupin, who I met in a bar in New York in the mid-1980s, and Daniel Lelong, who Jean introduced me to in Paris. He was sitting in his office, behind a large desk, and did not invite me in.

Frémon is described as being an important contributor to the "trans-genre tendency in contemporary French letters." Both he and Dupin were friends of the writer Marcel Cohen, who had written to me in the early 1980s, after receiving a copy of my book, *Broken Off by the Music* (1981), which had been published by Keith and Rosmarie Waldrop under their imprint, Burning Deck. In 1995, the Waldrops published Cohen's *The Peacock Emperor Moth,* short stories translated from the French by Cid Corman. This is how one reader described Cohen's work: "Here's how to write novels in two or three or four sentences. The headmaster of that strange school is Cohen." When I met Cohen, Frémon, and Dupin in Paris in the mid-1980s, they did not know that I had already met or been in contact with the others.

It was this series of orbits, which got me to meet Nicola, who is central to the story, though I don't believe the event I am referring to happened during this first visit. It was during another visit that he took me to a bar (or what Americans call a café) one afternoon. I know this didn't happen when we first met because the weather was warm and there was no snow on the ground.

It may have been on this trip that we drove outside of Turin to walk in the fields where Julius Caesar assembled his legions before crossing the Alps.

The choice was deliberate, as everything was with Nicola. He and the owner knew each other, though not well (it seemed to me). They spoke briefly, and introductions were made. I was presented as "poeta americano."

Nicola and I stood at the bar waiting for the owner to bring us our espressos. When he brought them over, he began speaking to me in passable English, asking if I knew of the poet, Cesare Pavese. As soon as I said, "yes," he pointed to an empty table in a separate room, by a small window and secluded from the other tables. "That is where Pavese and the American actress used to meet in the afternoons." He shook his head. "It all ended badly when she said, no," and said no more. At this, Nicola stiffened and became noticeably agitated. We finished our coffee in silence and left.

The owner never mentioned the actress's name, nor did Nicola tell me later, when we were walking to his studio. I only remember him saying "brutal," a word he used whenever he found something to be violent or ugly. In this case, he never said what exactly was "brutal" about this encounter, as he did when he shook his head and said of Pablo Picasso's and Jackson Pollock's paintings, "too brutal." He also expressed dissatisfaction with the owner, but I cannot remember what it was that so irked him. I think Nicola was offended by the owner's gossipy, concierge-like fascination with Pavese's suicide, but I am not sure. I do know that we never went back to that bar, even after I said that I wanted to talk to the owner again, as I was curious about the "American actress." Nicola's response made it clear that it was not a topic open for discussion. Was

De Maria, a devout Catholic, distressed because Pavese had committed suicide and that the owner had glorified it in some way?

De Maria had gotten a degree in medicine, with a specialization in psychiatry, but never practiced it. He was a self-taught artist whose life was changed when he met the artists Mario and Marisa Merz. After graduating, De Maria moved to Turin, where he began drawing and painting. He soon began painting directly on walls. In an interview he described himself as: "one who writes poems with his hands soaked in colors." In *Parole Cinesi*, De Maria made small colorful landscape abstractions, each of which he signed with the name of a Chinese artist. It is why I went to meet him.

I do not remember when I learned that the actress's name was Constance Dowling. I must have looked it up, but I don't remember doing this or when. In July 2014, in emails that I sent to Tom Nozkowski and John Ashbery, I mention Dowling, as I had recently seen her in *Blind Spot* (1947), which also starred Chester Morris and Steve Geray, and was directed by Robert Gordon, at the Museum of Modern Art's film series: *Lady in the Dark: Crime Films from Columbia Pictures, 1932–1957.* This was how the museum described the film:

> Taking a break from Columbia's Boston Blackie series, aging matinee idol Chester Morris stars as a vividly alcoholic author of pulp novels who falls under suspicion when his penny-pinching publisher is murdered by a method described in one of his stories. With a screenplay by Martin Goldsmith, the author of the novel that became Edgar G. Ulmer's *Detour*, this casually sordid, micro-budgeted noir features some inventive staging by the director Robert Gordon, including a one-shot, subjective camera scene strikingly similar to a famous sequence in Ulmer's film, as well as a rare sympathetic performance by the professional femme fatale Constance Dowling, whose romantic rejection of the Italian poet Cesare Pavese contributed to his suicide.

I think the program notes, and the mention of Dowling as "a professional femme fatale," which they never substantiated, was the only reason I went to see the film. According to the listing, I saw *Blind Spot* on July 21, 2014, at 6:45 p.m.

I told myself that the other reason I was going was because of Martin Goldsmith. *Detour* (1945), directed by Edgar G. Ulmer, and starring Tom Neal and Ann Savage, is one of my favorite noir films. In real life, the main actor Tom Neal had what De Maria would call a "brutal" temper and was later convicted of manslaughter. His career ended because of his relationship with the actress Barbara Payton, whose highpoint was starring with James Cagney in *Kiss Tomorrow Goodbye* (1950), and making 5,000 a week. That year, Payton met and became engaged to the actor Franchot Tone, while starting an affair with Tom Neal. Payton was very public about this triangle, which enraged Neal. On September 14, 1951, Neal, who had boxed while in college, physically attacked Tone at Payton's apartment, leaving Tone in an eighteen-hour coma with a smashed cheekbone, broken nose, and concussion. Even after she married Tone, Payton continued her affair with Neal, which led to Tone being granted a divorce in 1952. By 1951, Payton's star was losing its shine, as she starred in the low-budget horror *Bride of the Gorilla*, with Raymond Burr.

Neal's co-star, Ann Savage is hardly a sympathetic character, but her grating voice and acting are memorable, particularly because of lines, such as "Stop makin' noises like a husband."

Described as "The Meanest Woman in Film History" and as an "Unglamorous Psycho Villainess," Savage played forgettable roles in bad films for a decade (1943–1953) and is remembered only for being the hitchhiker, Vera, in *Detour*.

In 1985, Savage talked about her roles during the 1940s to the *Los Angeles Times*:

> They were mindless. The actresses were just scenery. The stories all revolved around the male actors; they really had the choice roles.

> All the actresses had to do was to look lovely, since the dialogue was ridiculous.

How did Dowling last as long as she did if she only gave unsympathetic performances? Isn't there something memorable about her besides her known effect on Pavese?

On July 31, 2014, Ashbery wrote back:

> I never heard of *Blind Spot*, and I must shamefully admit to not having heard of Constance Dowling either, though I of course know her sister, Doris, who was in Italian post-war neo-realist movies, e.g. *Bitter Rice*. We really should compare notes some time.

Later that day, I wrote to John:

> Doris is probably the reason Constance went to Italy. She also starred in some Italian neo-realist films. When I used to go to Turin to see a painter friend, we once had coffee in the shop where Pavese and Constance would meet. I just got *Black Angel* starring Dan Duryea, Peter Lorre and June Vincent (Dowling has a bit part), which Andrew Sarris considers one of the "25 most memorable cult films."

I think Sarris's description of *Black Angel* was why I wrote to Tom. Three years later, in an email dated January 17, 2017, I learned that in "March or April 1964," Nozkowski had dropped out of school, partly because he had just finished reading writings by Andrew Sarris that would appear in *The American Cinema: Directors and Directions 1929–1968*, a guide to over 200 film directors and an alphabetical listing of 6000 films, listing their directors and years they were released. When the book came out, Tom used it as a guide to directors and films he had not seen or taken seriously. After driving cross country and visiting friends in San Francisco and Los Angeles, and sharing a cabin with friends in Lowell, Vermont, he "came back to the city mid-Winter. The first order of business was to see Godard's *Contempt* which had just opened to the worst possible reviews and was sure to quickly disappear." Someone as dedicated to film as Tom was must have known about Constance Dowling, but I can find no comment from him about her or Doris in our extensive email correspondence.

I was wrong. Constance, who was Doris's older sister, moved to Rome first, hoping to revive her career. She had played female leads, but was starting to be moved further down the credits list. According to her IMDb biography,

> Once she started moving further down the credits list, as she was for the Republic film noir, *The Flame* (1947), which starred studio mogul Herbert J. Yates' wife Vera Ralston [who, I would add, was forty years younger than her husband], she decided to move to Italy and try and maintain her leading lady career there.

Ralston was born in Prague and had achieved modest success as a figure skater. She placed fifteenth in the 1936 European Figure Skating Championships and seventeenth in the 1936 Winter Olympics. According to Ralston, when Adolph Hitler asked her if she would like to "skate for the swastika," she told him that she would "rather skate on it." In Hollywood, because of her limited English skills, she normally played the part of a young immigrant woman. Because of her marriage to Yates, she was able to star in twenty movies, only two of which made money.

Constance's younger sister Doris, who by 1947 had achieved a modest degree of popularity, moved to Rome a short time later. I have seen a photo of Doris Dowling and Cesare Pavese standing together, but not one of Constance and him. Together, the Dowling sisters became the first American actresses to work exclusively in Italian films, which means they were bilingual, unlike Ralston. Her circle of friends included Alberto Moravia, Ernest Hemingway, Jean-Paul Sartre, and Robert Capa.

Constance never gained the attention that her sister Doris did, either in America or Italy. In 1946, the year before Constance starred in *Blind Spot*, "Bad Girl," an article by Frank Chapman, appeared on page 48 of the January 20, 1946 issue of *The Post-Standard*, a newspaper serving the metro area of Syracuse, New York:

> If Ray Milland's performance in the movie of Charlotte Jackson's *Lost Weekend* doesn't win him the Academy Award for 1945, then there is, of course, no hope for Hollywood. The Irish-born Monsoor Milland makes this teeth-rattling story of a drunk one of the tours de force of all time; he wraps up the picture and carries it home with him in the inside jacket pocket with the fifth of bourbon. Acting like that is knitted in the laps of the gods.
>
> Against this razzle-dazzle witchery, the neat but not gaudy efforts of players like Jane Wyman and Phil Terry are swallowed and forgotten—hopelessly swamped by the floodtide of emotion that Milland turns loose. But for a few memorable scenes—scenes that are tender and, Lord preserve us, poignant—Mr. Milland has some big league company. This is a dark-haired, high-cheekboned, sexotic piece of baggage named Doris Dowling—playing in the first movie she ever made in her life.

Chapman was right, of course, Milland won the Academy Award and Cannes Film Festival Award for his portrayal of an alcoholic writer in *Lost Weekend*. Later, in his profile of Doris, Chapman quotes her:

> The public may like the ingenues, but they remember the witches. I want to do a couple of those until I get my feet firmly on the ladder. In a way, I'm glad that Ray did such a terrific job in the first movie I made, because it sort of buries me and lets me climb slowly. If I were good enough to ring the bell the first time out and make the critics

click their heels, I'd be terrified—terrified that I couldn't live up to the inevitable buildup. That's happened not too long ago, you know.

Constance Dowling never got this kind of write-up. She got on the ladder as a second-liner in B films, because she was a "Goldwyn Girl," who was briefly favored by Samuel Goldwyn, before he turned his attention to Virgina Mayo. She was never able to climb higher or star in a breakthrough film. She never got to write her own ticket, as they say.

Constance previously had second billing with Chester Morris in *Boston Blackie and the Law* (1946), which was likely why they were paired again in *Blind Spot*. There is no on-screen magic between them, though this did not prevent Carole Lombard and Fred MacMurray from appearing in four films together at Paramount between 1935 and '37. According to Steve Vineberg, Distinguished Professor of the Arts and Humanities at the College of the Holy Cross in Worcester, Massachusetts, "It's easy to fall in love with [Lombard]; everything about her is endearing, including her nuttiness." No one ever described Dowling as endearing. In fact, there are almost no descriptions of her on-screen personality, her acting. It is almost as if she was not in the movies she was in.

After his relationship with Dowling ended, Pavese wrote in his diary:

> One does not kill oneself for love of a woman, but because love—any love—reveals us in our nakedness, our misery, our vulnerability, our nothingness.

In an essay that appeared in the *American Poetry Review* (September/October, 1997), Alan Williamson wrote:

> At first, Constance Dowling seemed the inconceivable remedy to this whole history of failure. Partly, it was simply because she was

> American. Pavese had long had a romance with what seemed to him the pragmatic yet innocent freshness in American culture; he had translated not only *Moby Dick* but many populist works of the twenties and thirties—Steinbeck, Sherwood Anderson, even Sinclair Lewis. At first he felt rejuvenated with Constance, restored to a self-confidence he did not know he possessed: "It was a terrible step, yet I took it. Her incredible sweetness, her 'Darlings,' her smile, her long-repeated pleasure at being with me. Nights at Cervinia, nights at Turin. She is a child, an unspoiled child. Yet she is herself—terrifying. From the bottom of my heart, I did not deserve so much." (16th March, 1950).

Not all went smoothly. One night, in Milan, Pavese told his biographer, Davide Lajolo:

> She fled at night from my bed at the hotel in Rome and she went to bed with another, with that actor you know. Like the other woman, even worse. Do you remember the one from Turin? She is the one who ended it between me and women.

Shortly after Constance turned down Pavese's marriage proposal and flew back to America, He wrote a poem in his diary that begins with a line (literally translated):

"Death Will Come and Will Have Your Eyes."

It will be the title of his final book of poetry, causing a scandal because two months after they separated, Pavese checked into a hotel in Turin and took a fatal overdose of sleeping pills.

The poem links love and morbidity.

Later on in the poem, Pavese writes,

It will be like ending a vice,
like seeing a dead face
emerge from the mirror,
like hearing closed lips speak.

Is this what it is like to sit in a dark auditorium and watch "lovely, exotic looking, hazel-eyed blonde Constance Dowling" appear on screen? She is never on screen long enough; the camera does not stare at her, even if there are those in the audience who want to.

The last film Dowling was in was the cult sci-fi flick, *Gog* (1954), about two robots, Gog and Magog in a secret underground laboratory in New Mexico, which are being controlled by an enemy robot plane. Dowling's role was to be a love interest and to scream. She was in her mid-thirties.

The independently made film was produced by Ivan Tors, who was interested in nonviolent science fiction movies and stories starring animals. His animal films include *Flipper* (1963), *Flipper's New Adventure* (1964), *Zebra in the Kitchen* (1965), but there is disagreement over whether he or his company produced *Clarence the Cross-Eyed Lion* (1965).

Tors and Dowling were married from 1955 to 1969, when she died of a heart attack at the age of forty-nine. They had four children, three of whom were in the film, *Escape from Angola* (1976). During the 1960s, she worked as a guide at the Dolphin Laboratory in St. Thomas, in the US Virgin Islands. She is buried at Holy Cross Cemetery, Culver City, California.

Doris Dowling's career took a different turn. She appeared in over sixty films, often typecast as wife, mother, old maid, busybody, aristocrat, gold digger, con artist, eccentric, femme fatale, landlady, neighbor, curmudgeon, reporter, secretary, nurse, politician, exotic, indigenous person, foreigner, doctor, clergywoman, retail clerk, businesswoman, and, in her later years, matriarch. She died in

2004, more than thirty years after Constance, and is also interred at Holy Cross Cemetery.

A few days ago, I began this piece after reading Doug Lang's sonnet, "Unheard Melodies Endure," which contains the line: "Cesare Pavese loved Constance Dowling."

It was like reading graffiti on a wall somewhere, a testament that someone had left behind.

Section 7
(2024)

Morning Notes I–X

I.

I wake up and think I am still alive
but there is no guarantee
it will last to sunset,
just you wait and see
I tell myself
Sometimes I listen to what I am saying

II.

I like to think I give good advice, but this is one of the many lies
I tell myself I should forget but can't, at least until it starts snowing
The last time it snowed the sun was shining
The weather will become colder each spring,
things are changing, we waited and watched,
it isn't a movie. Happy endings are a thing of the past,
like telephone booths and saluting a flag

III.

I drink black coffee from a blue cauldron
I forget stairs can go in two directions
Who said I was going anywhere
I am already nowhere in sight

IV.

Better luck next time
and the time after that, and so on
Do you have anything to bargain with
besides the monkey on your back

V.

You got to beat the hills into shape,
good shape, otherwise nature
gets to keep the upper hand
You will live to regret this
or if not this
then this and this and that
Something has got to give

VI.

I keep hearing that one in the hand
is worth less than it used to be

VII.

You could say that I am an all-you-want-on-it-burger
without leftover meat, this is not a joke pretending
to be a fire drill, elephants recently took up residence in my brain
Just because you can't see them, doesn't mean they are not there

VIII.

I can no longer explain the difference between right and wrong
now that my left hand is a separate entity
a loss to cojoined obligations, doing whatever it wants
Damp barriers at the local dump, give me back my polluted pen
my instrument of nostril soot dripping drunken ant scratches

IX.

When someone tried to return
my identity, I told them
they could keep it,
as I had another door
hidden in my frontal globe

X.

You have to seize the iron handkerchief
wipe the ants from your green brow

This is how you pretend
to be only the air you breathe

Cento for David Shapiro

1) O Lord, thou didn't pluck me out too cleanly

2) I wrote this poem for you and haven't lost it

3) The voice is a wandering part of the body

4) One word tied to another—that is all
You know. No cherry blossoms.

5) I always loved to climb that ladder without rungs, I collect them.
I fight over them, I forgive

6) When a poet is weak,
like a broken microphone,
he still has some power,
indicated by a red light

7) Aren't we the lucky ones?

8) If there were the right word for everything, each young philosopher
could dream without sleeping.

9) On very few days has it stopped snowing in my sleep.

10) Involuntary
        memory as in Proust
        is more than I can bear

11) Certain poets who seem to be crazy let out a radical thin filament of joy, and this is enough.

12) Yes, I'm me and I refuse to make a poem into a competitive sport.

13) All I need is a clean desk.

14) I remember reading of wanting to read all of Dickens and then all of Nietzsche
There is a tremendous sadness in all this.
So I say it again: Only a person who forgets what it means to read ever says he has read all of Quixote or all of Borges.

15) I cannot imagine art without vision, dreams, the oneiric.

16) *The Tale of Genji* is a folded dream.

17) Could it be you know I am still living, leashed to the hateful sky

18) When Allen walking around Weequahic Lake with me said but can you memorize John Ashbery's poetry, I proudly recited from some of the most incomprehensible poems (Night). When it was over, Allen beamed and said incomprehensibly, Oh I get it, it's like Alexander Pope.

19) I too grew up in
the soft hands
of the gods

20) Often best: the albatross and no explanation given.

21) Give me a first line, you who are far away.
The second line will almost write itself.
In times of pain, I open the dictionary.

22) Practice or you'll eat
In the garage
With the dog

23) I could use 100 years of cello lessons from CASALS. CASALS SAID ONLY A DONKEY NEEDS MORE THAN 3 HOURS A DAY, I am that donkey

24) You sat alone in a corner of the page

25) The day was full of day
On Exterior Street
Moths drank tears from sleeping birds

26) You in rayon with your ton of discs frisk in the garden

27) Should we make love or translate? Is there a more beautiful sentence than that you have read in the last century: Shall we make love or translate? You will find a few friends in this world, but not many sentences as beautiful as that question, which makes one love questions?

28) I agree, who can live for long without string quartets?

29) Give me a first line, you who are far away.
The second line will almost write itself.
In times of pain, I open the dictionary.

30) At night, you burn like the library of Alexandria.

31) In the morning you are Alexandria, in a mirror.
You are so black you are white, like a firefly in sunlight.

32) Without the organ or piano I could not really become a composer the way I wanted.

33) Rilke's letters are often disgusting

34) Isn't it wonderful that Shakespeare shut up.

35) Keats's are the best letters—he wants to know how Shakespeare sat—aren't we lucky not to know.

36) Yes, Valéry is an abyss of thought wrecking itself.

37) The Dalai Lama says he could remember every breath he takes, though it would be a certain effort. He knows his past either like Proust or like the Goncourt brothers. I would be interested in his memoirs, the long version.

38) I guess saints should write their memoirs, but it's obvious why they don't.

39) Even Picasso can be whimsical.

40) I can't understand calculus, and it's unlikely that I will ever understand Leibniz. But I do remember your face.

41) I think of my translation of
Baudelaire's *Luxe, calme, et volupté*
Rich calm and open

42) They say Lady Day called it her song. It is that moment when it is all of our songs.

43) And how many
will have their last books published
as if the Lord published them
and the young poets will be howling for their skin?

44) That night I saw a fountain
inscribed with this advice:
Laugh loudly love as my voice laughs in the gray water.

45) Clark Coolidge met Juan Gris bumping into Ron Padgett

46) How wonderful to be in the arms of cerebral creatures

47) To you who carried me like mail from one house to another
To wild flesh

48) The only emperor is yours; I'm just taking dictation.

49) To leave
    The world alone, largely uninterpreted
    For the wet pavement
    On which he may scratch his poems

50) In the desert of the desert, you have left a trace.

51) I asked my mother for a new form from Paradise. All I saw was a sestina in lines of color.

52) So if a person loves you they might say
I want to be in Hell with you forever

53) I am drawing your outline now by memory,
a quiet game that is always a way

and I am trying to place the lakes, rivers and life's dust within a few miles of where they belong

54) I too hated aspects of my family, that novel, but I used poetry to place that hate in a secret strong place.

55) My mind is on my mind. But when I let it go, I can post true pencils.

56) Give me my arrow's desire.

57) "I am a girl from a poor family and it has taken me a long time to make these silk clothes . . . And these I will no longer wear . . . And I am wiping the lipstick from my lips . . . etc."

58) Patient in love and in death, a satisfied ghost

59) The best letters I have received are Fairfield Porter's and they are noble as Whitehead. Now all we need are poems as dry and noble, informative and delightful as one detail of light.

60) Lightly you touch me
paper on which I write
Problems have turned into snow at night
like a little car abandoned in the midst of vague terror

61) FOR A MOMENT GOD DOES NOT EXIST

62) IN A FOLD IN A WHITE MODERATE MORNING AT THEIR END OF ENDINGS

63) Kenneth taught me how to make homemade mayonnaise. I had never thought it was necessary or even interesting.

64) I still recall asking Fairfield Porter: How can I paint in the past tense?

65) Mondrian liked many dances, but most of all the ones where we do not touch.

66) Certain mysteries are almost interesting: Lewis Carroll.

67) They say I may hallucinate soon
I will have to discriminate between
my friend the squirrel my love the rat

68) Sparkling and traveling without luggage

69) Ordinary unhappiness is a long poem

70) How come poets think only their style will do, when a thousand orchids splash.

71) A kit of my poems secretly comes from memorizing lucid dreams. I began to be able to memorize about sixteen lines in a dream. I didn't want to tell people, because it seemed a bit Californian

72) But I do love when poems are GIVEN to me in my dreams. I feel as if I wake up and have already worked.

73) Once when I told JJ that Russel had said he was the best American painter, he said: Is that all I am?

74) You who think fame is interesting might brood upon the Oscars.

75) I am a poet only a poet
and I am no better than any other poet
and no poet is better than me.

76) Wild coca-cola is difficult to find.

77) I remember every merciless thing you said in the spirit of a photo album waking from the dead—

78) New theory of the violin, that the bigger the hole the better the tone

79) May those dying start to live again in ways in which doctors can't possibly comprehend

80) I am dreaming of a house with a thousand windows and a million doors, I would like to house there all the poor poets of the world . . . If I could only see this temple before my eyes, I would die of exhaustion, die frozen, but still satisfied . . . . . .

81) Dost thou expect me to be amazed by the simple sullen reiteration of old things.

82) Could it be you know I am still living, leashed to the hateful sky

83) Less and less mind, like that child taking Greyhound buses across American deserts so he could bottle the Pacific for a second—

84) I'm exhausted by Parkinson's, but even thinking of Sacco and Ethel rejuvenates me.

85) That's fair and Frank O'Hara leaps into the waves.

86) I FELT HIS ESSENTIAL LONELINESS.

87) Did Miller know that one day she would be a great war journalist and bathe in Hitler's tub

88) I am on your mind, how you would retype my poems on special paper. I regarded that as the peak of love.

89) What's on your mind. Whether I am ever on your mind.
Is that a song friends or just a friendly post.

90) I too hated aspects of my family, that novel, but I used poetry to place that hate in a secret strong place.

91) I would like to comb

the haiku from your hair

vertical braid of language necklace of

words pinprick of a single sound

92) I asked my mother for a new form from Paradise. All I saw was a sestina in lines of color.

93) She crosses the street to say
I will be afraid for both of us.

94) This too had a pedestal
or place or double door
or triple tomb

95) Kenneth Koch once told me that in certain countries Ron Padgett would be an ambassador. (We both knew I wouldn't last for three weeks.)

96) Maps of the present fall from me
with exits entrances names of the judges, the judged

97) A certain violinist had a beautiful violin

98) And so the snow fell and covered up poetry

99) In one day how much can a doctor destroy, how much can a poet keep fresh?

100) Death is just a long snow day

For Brice Marden (1938–2023) via Han Shan

My paintings are made in a highly subjective state within Spartan limitations
I chose a distant place to dwell, a garden you can visit when I am not there

Sometime scholar, artist, and poet, I collect rocks and sing lullabies to butterflies
The snow will bury my body. Will it matter who reads my work when I am gone

I chose a distant place to dwell, a garden you can visit when I am not there
I paint as I see and feel, and I have very strong feelings

The snow will bury my body. Will it matter who reads my work when I am gone
My only joy is poetry, scribbling and scribbling until my brain falls out

I paint as I see and feel, and I have very strong feelings
People ask the way to my studio. I tell them I am a chameleon

My only joy is poetry, scribbling and scribbling until my brain falls out
I work with the illusion of light. My heart's not the same as yours

People ask the way to my studio. I tell them I am a chameleon
My paintings are made in a highly subjective state within Spartan limitations.

I work with the illusion of light. My heart's not the same as yours
Sometime scholar, artist, and poet, I collect rocks and sing lullabies to butterflies

Documentary Cinema

Money moves the herd, divides the nods from the hard-nosed, keeps others lacquered shut. Occasionally, unexpected turbulence from a recalcitrant stump lantern introduces confusion, but these interruptions are not unexpected and easily papered over. While across the aisle, another globe sets off sparks. What animal do you most resemble when you are not an armadillo, surrounded by sordid ornaments, sweaty to the touch? Tender bellow mortified by fat. Postcard gargoyle in need of a second bath. Mouth full of severed thumbs. Pauses in leaky silence, station changes, climb into latest examples of a ruined civilization, what we call the present. Moon pasted frozen bright on wall near names of repeatedly missing. Adjacent to commuter clatter, some filled with hard eyes. Wheel cover pandering to paper blocks, championing virtues of carbon trash, rods circulating cups on ice, another bleeding sky cools at its own pace.

Silent Film Without Music

What if you watched a movie in a language that you don't understand and are asked to communicate the plot to someone who has never grasped what you are saying, said the poet, laughing at a familiar predicament. The faces and feet offer no clues. Suppose talking about the movie reminds you of the first person whose tongue touched yours and said kissing is like rolling little migraine pillows around on the floor when no one is looking, and that being in love is like trying to understand a silent movie that no one has ever described accurately. All that exists are the pages upon pages of words that have been written about it, bound in embossed and numbered volumes. What has puzzled the scholars who have pored over these tomes is that each description denies the existence of all the others, so that one has never been able to summarize the plot or lack of one, fragments of fragments, some of them marked only by the shadows of clouds that were in the sky that day, not so long ago, before memory had become a phantom limb.

A Be Sky

for Barry Schwabsky and Carol Szymanski

Aleph begat silver kelp yesterday
Bodacious commanded Tobias lop zillions
Creighton disrupts understanding masterful abrogation
Dirtbag evidence values nimble beefsteak
Evelyn frees woebegone orangutan committee
Frederick grabs x-ray pamphlet directions
Gertrude hovers yonder querulous envoy
Hornswoggle invites zircon realtor's fancy
Indigo Jones apprehends summer grubstake
Judson kills bodily trapped haloes
Kiefer loves crummy underwear indicators
Lulu manhandles determined value jumpers
Mason neutralizes ethereal warden's keystone
Nathan outwardly freezes xanthochroous leaves
Oscar pumps goaded Yankee money
Petrus quacked holy zinnia nubs
Quagmire rotted indigo apple obbligato
Rusty studies jodhpur brown pacemakers
Stefania trampoline kicks cabalist quorum
Thomas übermensch lambastes drapery reception
Underwood verifies macerated Edwardian Samaritans
Vera wails noxious furry tomorrow
Wally's xiphiplastron operates garbled ultimatums
Xanthippe yells phony harridan validations
Young zealot questions irradiated waffles

Aging Elfin Blues

Bald and on brink of evaporation
I climb onto latest spotted mushroom
to rise out of black loam
and ding out a few trembling bars . . .

I am not sure why I needed to write this down. Nearly everyone who was there is dead or locked away in a tinny bin, where no one gets tucked in at night. Nix velvet caps with cowbells. Next time bring a bow and an arrow or two. Remember to wash your glittery socks, one in each hand, in a sink big enough to cup a baby sparrow. And don't wear that awful blue bow tie, I was told. But, as these things go, I failed to listen, and all records of my participation were expunged. You cannot change history even after it changes you. Believe that and you will be spotted wearing a hard hat the next time you go to the bathroom under a full moon.

Have you reached that point in your life where you are unable to hear the latest round of thunderstorms brewing in the refrigerator?

What kind of hogwash is this if you can't rinse off the family pig?

I tried to tell you that forgetting is the shortest route to fame, but you were too busy listening to the other broadcast, the one full of rushing waters, skies bathed in horrid colors. What if post-zombie gas stations become a popular tourist destination? Will that mean we won? At certain moments any wonder will do. Doesn't everyone still dream of stopping for another refill, even if they are loathe to admit it?

A Voice in the Studio of Peter Paul Rubens

Are these bloated corpses or pink sunlit clouds—no one can decide
Whether outfitted in smart attire, traditional outfits, or athletic gear

When will you draw the bitterness inflaming our upturned faces
Tell us which chariot will measure the daily turmoil

Whether outfitted in smart attire, traditional outfits, or athletic gear
We will lean on past arguments, whose expiration date has come and gone

Tell us which chariot will measure the daily turmoil
Who among us can respond patiently to the litany of anonymous complaints

We will lean on past arguments, whose expiration date has come and gone
While a texture of devastation shuttles its multicolored threads throughout the day

Who among us can respond patiently to the litany of anonymous complaints
The distribution of wealth is not about delivering buckets of money

While a texture of devastation shuttles its multicolored threads throughout the day
I decide to wear a tuxedo complete with glossy pompadour and fly into the sun

The distribution of wealth is not about delivering buckets of money
Our ugliness preceded us like a mirror held up to the assembling wind

Are these bloated corpses or pink sunlit clouds—no one can decide
I decide to wear a tuxedo complete with glossy pompadour and fly into the sun

Our ugliness preceded us like a mirror held up to the assembling wind
When will you draw the bitterness inflaming our upturned faces

Diary of Small Discontents

1) The movie did not stay with me. In fact, it was never there.

2) Later, when I realized the animals suspended all forms of broadcasting, I stopped sending messages via the usual channels. As the poet dwindled further into the sour, he began making gnomic pronouncements: a bird in the hand, it takes two, you just can't. Students copied the statements into spiral notebooks, speculated on what was left out and why. Whirlpools of wind swirled down the street, lifting and dropping insects whose spirits had departed.

3) You just can't pay less than full attention to huts made with a radial arm saw.

4) Returned to lab. Went straight there from drugstore. Walked under rubber clouds. Found series of inappropriate messages delivered to electronic mailbox. Warning shots fired. As information highway becomes increasingly crowded with squatters, the odds of shopping malls squeezed between prison complexes and gated communities multiply like fungi after rain. Have you ever thought about the fluorocarbons lurking in your spaghetti?

5) Sobbing church bell breadstick complications.

6) Dancing with skin, flotilla of small scars continuously changes shape. As weeks pass, busboy thickens. Flasher flicks make brief comeback on outer fringes of suburbs. There are so many different kinds of Asians living in New York it is getting harder to tell them apart.

7) Soon to be a major emotional picture.

8) A sea of bobbing pink umbrellas floods the plaza. It is proving difficult to align outer carapace with inner substance. Kulaks and kayaks drift apart in commercial. Stop waffling over your waffles, my little alphabet

9) Full disclosure is a come-on.

10) Went up to the coffin and kissed your cold lips good-bye. Memory of that moment returns unexpectedly while staring at computer screen. Younger brother doing the same thing. Woman who needed to be hoisted up the stairs. Talking to people who told a story rather than their names. Father counting the bouquets, wondering if he will have as many when his time comes.

11) Remember, the brain is not a safe place to think.

Memories of Charles Street, Boston

1.

One day I wake up and my hair has turned white
and I am no longer Chinese.

I want to ask my mother about this change in my appearance
but she has been dead longer than I have been alive.

You have to take the good with the bad she used to tell me
before trying to drown me in the bathtub.

My father sat in the next room in his imported black underwear,
smoking a perfumed cigar, and jerking off

in front of the television that he had dragged in from the street.
It never worked. It still doesn't, and the blue stains on the chair

are why I never sit there.

2.

My mother, if that
was what she was
told me drowning
was the most
efficient way
to leave the house,
no footprints,

hard to trace
never before

My mother told me
I must drown you
my idiot child
my beloved offspring
my grievance
I am giving you
my only chance
to breathe water smoothly
to swim away
from this couch
where death awaits you

3.

You will grow up
my mother said
you will be a poet
when you grow up
not a beanstalk
like the fortune teller told me
A poet who ties words together
one sound adhered to the next
This is the music you will sing
to an empty hall or crowded hell
to a room full of eager beavers
You will grow up and be a poet
singing songs, singing and wringing
no one will listen to you
just as you never listened to me

my mother said to a vacant room
blind at the end of the darkness
she had pulled down around her

4.

When I asked my mother
why I didn't speak Chinese
she said when you were a baby
you refused to learn it
What about English
You refused to learn that too

5.

I hear my father
smiling on the phone

Just before your mother
crashed down the stairs

from a stroke
you likely caused

she said
the fortune teller had been all wrong

nothing of what he said about my son
had turned out true

6.

My father said
the plane flew
without fuel

like a bird
riding waves of sunlight
streaming through its windows

7.

My father loved to leave me
in a movie theater
by myself
beginning when I was six

seated alone
by the aisle

He paid the usher a dime
to make sure
no one kidnapped or molested me

Michael Ansara, Jeff Chandler, and Ruth Roman
were my cartoon heroes
living and dying in a gray world
in a double-feature
all glamor gone in their second run.

My father hated me and told me so
in so many ways
I have almost lost count

The last time
was when he was at home
dying

The growth had become a ball
stuck inside him
and swelling

When I brought him medicine
to relieve the pain
he said

"You're too stupid to give me those
I will wait for your brother to come home"

Acknowledgments

I would like to thank my first readers: Albert Mobilio, Andrew Joron, Anselm Berrigan, Joseph Donahue, Laura Mullen, Michael Leong, and Peter Gizzi.

The poems in this book have previously appeared in the following books and chapbooks:

The Reading of an Ever-Changing Tale (Nobodaddy Press, 1977); *Sometimes* (Sheep Meadow Press, 1979); *Broken Off by the Music* (Burning Deck, 1981); *Corpse and Mirror* (Holt, Rinehart and Winston, 1983): *Radiant Silhouette: New & Selected Work 1974–1988* (Black Sparrow Press, 1989); *Big City Primer: Reading New York at the End of the Twentieth Century*, Photographs by Bill Barrette (Timken Publishers, 1991); *Edificio Sayonara* (Black Sparrow, 1992); *Berlin Diptychon*, Photographs by Bill Barrette (Timken Publishers, 1995); *Forbidden Entries* (Black Sparrow, 1996); *Borrowed Love Poems* (Penguin Books, 2002); *Ing Grish*, Art by Thomas Nozkowski (Saturnalia Books, 2005); *Paradiso Diaspora* (Penguin Books, 2006); *Further Adventures in Monochrome* (Copper Canyon, 2012); *Egyptian Sonnets* (Rain Taxi, 2012); *Annals of a Gumshoe,* Art by Trevor Winkfield (Smoke Specs, 2019); *Catullus Sails to China* (Olchef Press, 2020); *Genghis Chan on Drums* (Omnidawn, 2021); *Elsa and Charles with Cameo by Tallulah* (Earthbound Poetry Series, London, UK, 2022), *Tell It Slant* (Omnidawn, 2023).

"Cameo of a Chinese Woman on Mulberry Street" was first published as a postcard by Bellevue Press (1974)

"Russian Letter (3)" was first published as a broadside by the Dia Art Foundation (1999)

"Broken Sonnet" was first published as a broadside, designed and printed by Nancy Loeber (Center for Book Arts, 2003)

"Confessions of a Recycled Shopping Bag" was first published as a broadside, designed and printed by Alisa Ochoa (Center for Book Arts, 2011)

"Epithalamium" was first published as a broadside, designed and printed by Les Ferris (Black Square Editions, 2011) for the wedding of Benjamin La Rocco and Linnea Paskow on May 30, 2011

"Inuit Villanelle" was first published as "Eskimo Villanelle" for an exhibition by John Lees at Compass/Rose (Chicago, 1989)

The poems in *Section 7* (2024) have appeared in the following magazines:

Chicago Review (online), *Conjunctions*, *Kenyon Review*, *Posit*, *The Baffler*, *Vestiges*.

About the Author

John Yau is the author of many books, including, most recently, a selection of essays, *Please Wait by the Coatroom: Reconsidering Race and Identity in American Art* (Black Sparrow, 2023), a monograph, *Joe Brainard: the Art of the Personal* (Rizzoli Electa, 2022), and a volume of poetry, *Tell It Slant* (Omnidawn, 2023). He received the 2018 Jackson Poetry Prize, a Rabkin Award for his art criticism in 2021, and the Culture-Warren Award for poetry from the Hunan Academy of Poetry in 2022. He lives and works in Beacon, New York.

Diary of Small Discontents: New & Selected Poems 1974–2024
by John Yau

Cover design by Shanna Compton
Cover typeface: Museo Sans
Interior design by Shanna Compton
Interior typefaces: Adobe Garamond Pro & Museo Sans

Printed in the United States
by Books International, Dulles, Virginia
on Acid-Free Archival Quality Recycled Paper

Publication of this book was made possible in part by gifts from
Katherine & John Gravendyk in honor of Hillary Gravendyk,
Francesca Bell, Mary Mackey, and The New Place Fund

Omnidawn Publishing Oakland, California
Staff and Volunteers, Fall 2025
Rusty Morrison & Laura Joakimson, co-publishers
Elizabeth Aeschliman, production editor
Sophia Carr, production editor
Rob Hendricks, poetry & fiction editor
Jeffrey Kingman, copy editor
Hazel White, copy editor
Sharon Zetter, poetry editor & book designer
Anthony Cody, poetry editor
Liza Flum, poetry editor
Jennifer Metsker, marketing assistant
Avantika Chitturi, marketing assistant
Angela Liu, marketing assistant

www.ingramcontent.com/pod-product-compliance
Lightning Source LLC
Chambersburg PA
CBHW031425150426
43191CB00006B/397
* 9 7 8 1 6 3 2 4 3 1 7 5 2 *